June 8, 1997

Emily,
   I picked book store. [...] about it, but I thought you might find it kind of interesting. I read the first few pages and it seemed alright. So maybe bring this on the plane with you and read a story or two. I felt it was fitting because of the title. Just like everyone always says, this is the first step in the rest of our lives. Someone else once said something like, "Partings create such sorrow." I will miss you next year. You are a special person to me! Please keep in touch and have fun in Germany!
            Love you,
              Jenny

PARTINGS
And Other Beginnings

BOOKS BY RUTH RUDNER

Wandering

Huts and Hikes in the Dolomites

Off & Walking

Forgotten Pleasures

*Bitterroot to Beartooth:
Hiking Southwest Montana*

Greetings from Wisdom, Montana

PARTINGS

And Other Beginnings

by

RUTH RUDNER

CONTINUUM • NEW YORK

1993

The Continuum Publishing Company
370 Lexington Avenue
New York, NY 10017

COPYRIGHT © 1993 BY RUTH RUDNER

All rights reserved. No part of this book may be reproduced, stored in a retrieval system, or transmitted, in any form or by any means, electronic, mechanical, photocopying, recording, or otherwise, without the written permission of The Continuum Publishing Company.

Printed in the United States of America

Library of Congress Cataloging-in-Publication Data

Rudner, Ruth.
    Partings : and other beginnings / by Ruth Rudner.
       p. cm. — (Chronicles of transformation)
    ISBN 0-8264-0629-7
    1. Spirituality. 2. Conversion. I. Title. II. Series.
BL624.R7933   1993
814'.54—dc20   93-31769
                                                                             CIP

For SONYA HUDSON and AL RUDNER
my mother and father

Acknowledgements

Many of these chapters had their genesis in articles written for the Leisure & Arts Page of *The Wall Street Journal.*

There are thanks due: To Bruce Detrick, for reading and editing this manuscript, for his invaluable help, his love, belief, friendship; for the inspiration of his music; for the pleasure of his company, even when it is 2,000 miles away. To Marty Luray, for the nurturing thoughts he gave to everything I wrote. To Barbara Honeyman, for taking the care and time with this manuscript that allowed me to see what was there. To my editor Rob Baker, for his enormous kindness.

Contents

Monte Alban   1
The Warmth of a Stone
   Lying in the Path   10
The Train   18
Oaxaca   20
Blue   26
After the Horse Died   39
Poet   45
Winter   55
Flowers   63
Meadow   74
Ms. Lillian's Bookstore   80
Esther   91
The Big Drive   95
Cedar Key   105
The North American Open   108
The Christmas Bird   118
Takashi   123
Afterword   129

Monte Alban

The plane flies over snow-covered Popocatépetl and Iztaccihuatl on its way from Mexico City to Oaxaca. It lands at Oaxaca airport in the hot afternoon. Deep blue with scudding white clouds, the sky presses down on the steep green mountains edging the star-shaped valley of Oaxaca. The mountains have the jagged shape of Rockies or Alps, but they are covered by trees. There is nothing here like Popocatépetl. I find the intensity of green oppressive. I long for what is open, bare; for high mountains, deserts, oceans; all the places one can see forever. I long to see forever.

    I am not curious about Oaxaca, eager as I am to get to Wyoming and the Wind River Range, which I will do in July. We have agreed that I will spend six weeks in Oaxaca, then leave for Wyoming. My husband will stay through the summer. He has been to Oaxaca. He spent three weeks there this past winter, visiting our friends Genie and Joe Patrick, painters, on sabbatical from Iowa State, where they both teach. It was the first time in our seventeen years of marriage we had been apart because he had gone somewhere. I was always the one who traveled. While he was there he lost the gold chain I bought him a long time ago in Austria. It had a small gold medallion on it, engraved to him from me with love.

My husband drives our rented Volkswagen around the edges of the city of Oaxaca, then up the valley. Dogs amble along the two-lane highway lined with fields of maguey, the huge blue-green swirls of spiny fronds rising up row after row, mile after mile. Every so often we pass a dead dog. Goats, cows and burros are tethered to narrow patches of roadside green. Dirt roads branch off the highway, stretching long, difficult miles into remote mountain villages. At each intersection Indians gather, waiting for the valley bus to take them into the city, or to another intersection, from which they will walk miles to another village. The women, dressed in cotton house-dresses and, over them, printed cotton aprons, shade themselves from the inexorable sun with dark shawls draped over their heads and shoulders. They have always done this. When they have babies, they make slings out of the shawls to carry their babies. They balance baskets on their heads, the baskets containing tortillas or dishes or corn. Most are barefoot. So are most of the men.

I am drawn by the people in this landscape. I see them as rooted in it, the way the big trees and the gullies are rooted in it; the way the cultivated fields and dead dogs, the long miles of bad roads and the extravagance of flowers massed against the walls of houses are rooted in it. Maybe it's being barefoot. You touch the earth when you are barefoot. You grasp it with your toes, press it with your heel, the ball of your foot. You feel what the earth feels like. The people standing at the intersections neither talk nor smile. The women stand wrapped in the mystery of their shawls. I long for shawls to wrap around me, as if the shawls would root me to the earth. I forget I had no wish to come here. I merely long to be rooted. I long to hear how the language of these people sounds when they speak with one another. I long to know of what they speak.

About twenty minutes from town, we turn off the highway onto a dirt road. The road climbs steeply up through the villages of San Miguel and San Gabriel, becoming more and more rutted, its dirt washed away by years of rainy seasons. At its steepest part, there is no dirt at all. The road is used mostly by burros and travelers on foot. Nobody in the government really cares about village roads unless they lead to ruins. The Volkswagen, in first gear, climbs rocks.

In the villages we catch sudden glimpses through the open gates of walled courtyards of verandas draped with the flamboyant oranges, reds and pinks of bougainvillea; of women, children, pigs and chickens all in constant motion while odd mixtures of dogs lie lazily in the dust or against the cool sides of adobe houses.

The people we pass stop to stare at us. Some call out *Adios*. The greeting draws me further into the landscape because I hear it as a benediction. Perhaps all greetings are benedictions, blessings on one's presence. If you are greeted, it must be all right to be where you are. Yet, there are so many who only stare. *Adios,* we answer back, grateful.

At the edge of the higher village, about five miles, and twenty minutes, from the highway, we turn onto a car track leading further uphill to El Molina, an eighteenth century mill converted to a small hotel by Americans Rex and Lolly Marcum. The Marcums have lived in Mexico twenty-five years. Rex is from Wyoming. I am going to Wyoming, but Wyoming is right here. It is probably true that everything one wants is always where one is. How much we move must be a measure of how much we want, or of how our desires change. My husband has been writing to the Marcums for months to make arrangements to rent from them the seventeenth century mill they own not far from the hotel. It has survived three centuries of earthquakes and volcanoes. Moving into it the following morning, after spending the night in one of the beautiful rooms of the Marcums' hotel, we dust the chairs free of a thick layer of volcanic ash. The chairs have not been used since the last eruption a few months earlier.

The mill consists of a long, broad room of white brick, a wooden, beamed ceiling and broad plank floors with huge windows of small panes extending along both sides of the room and along one end. The windows give onto a view of mountains and fields and immense sky. Down three steps, there is a smaller, tile-floored room with a door opening onto a narrow balcony and a window over a sink. The window and the sink are exactly centered over the stream that once ran the mill so that when I wash my face it seems as if I am washing in the stream.

There is a kitchen sink and a stove in the main room. The whole place is furnished with nothing more than some wooden tables and chairs, a narrow bench, two beds made of wood, a few lamps and a few kerosene lamps for when the electricity goes out in a storm. It is all we need. It is beautiful. Next to the sink is an enormous jug of water which must be used for everything and, although it is filtered, must still be boiled to drink. When the jug is empty, Rex will bring us another.

The air at the mill smells of the bougainvillea that grows against its walls, and of the cows in the fields below. The rolling fields are the scenes in Genie Patrick's paintings. I was never entranced by her paintings, only

Partings

because the landscape was never my landscape. It is neither a joyous landscape nor a dramatic one, although I cannot say what it lacks in joy. It is built of shades of undulating green, one softly edging the next in a gentle geometry that is somehow, under the hot sky, ominous. Perhaps it is simply knowing that Mexico's lushness masks its extremes of cruelty. In a country of extremes, this particular landscape presents itself as a mediator, a kind of pastoral dream. One thinks land does not lie, yet here, in Oaxaca, it does. Without having been in Oaxaca, I think I felt that in Genie's paintings. Yet now, in the Oaxaquenian landscape, I see it differently. I look at the land and see her paintings and I am awed by what she has painted. It is so beautiful that I forget we have come here to part.

We have not spoken of our parting, yet it is something we each know. We have spoken only of the fact that this is a place for my husband to paint. The colors, the light of Mexico, the amazing, hard, all-consuming, violent beauty of it is, without question, a place for him to paint. Even in this pastoral landscape surrounding the mill, I feel some underlying violence. Perhaps it is history I feel; the brutality of Mexico's history. Perhaps history only mirrors the brutality of this earth that heaves and breaks and spews out lava and ash and fills the soul with the darkness of jungles and the dry brilliance of the sun. My husband will paint the color and light of this land. I have seen the color and light and tragic beauty of it in other places in Mexico, but nothing prepares me for this intensity of place. Oaxaca is different than other parts of Mexico. There is a sense, in Oaxaca, that, although it had its colonial period, and there are colonial buildings in the city, the colonial never took hold over the Indian—Olmtec, Zapotec, Mixtec. Part of what I sense in

Oaxaca is something I can never quite know; and part is the depths of its sorrow.

The unknowable, the incomprehensible, the sorrow, color and light. These are what draw my husband here. This is what he can paint. This is what joins us in this place. We are together in it. We are good at these things.

The Marcums bring food for dinner our first night at the mill. We sit at the old wooden table, seduced by the beauty of the mill into believing we could stay forever. My husband feels we are not so much parting as redefining our relationship on something other than sexual terms. It has always been on something other, but unspoken, the pressures were, for him, unbearable. Now that he has freed himself of that pressure he feels we are free to follow our own lives. Whether we come together again or not is, for him, both possible and beside the point. The point for him is that we get on with our lives separately, but backed up, forever, by the knowledge of, and experience of, the closeness of our friendship. I suppose I agree. And I suppose that's more security than most people ever have. From this point, then, I should be able to find my own way.

When we speak, we do not speak of these things. We have spoken of them already. We have spoken of them enough. We do not need to speak of them. When we speak, we speak of Oaxaca. We concentrate on ruins...Monte Alban, Yagul, Mitla...enthralled by all that is ancient, yet available to our presence. We are together in these places. We are alone. It's how we have always been. What we shared—our wonder at finding ourselves not alone—was usually more powerful than our aloneness. We felt such pride in our sharing, as if it set us apart from the rest of the world.

Pride, of course, is a sin. And sin is trouble. Although neither of us come from backgrounds that concern themselves with sin, we probably will never entirely extricate ourselves from the Greater Culture and its constant fiddling around with sin. Some notion of sin—philosophical or religious or psychological—seems always to be hovering in the atmosphere like a virus. Everyone, however healthy, is occasionally vulnerable to a virus.

We were so proud of us, we thought we should exist together as some sort of example to the world that a shared life is, indeed, possible. It was like staying alive. For a period of time our friends kept dying, most of them before they were forty. They weren't even dying of AIDS. They were just dying. We felt we had an obligation to stay alive; to show it could be done. The same thing happened when all those who hadn't died began getting divorced. We felt we had an obligation to stay together. It was up to us to stay both alive and married so the world would see such things were possible.

It is appropriate that we are so beguiled by ruins; the leftover places that, holding their private histories among their public stones, present to those who visit moods that can be entered; memories that can be invented. Given our view of ourselves, it was not odd that we were most intrigued by Monte Alban. It was, after all, the most grand.

On a series of hills thirteen hundred feet above the valley floor, Monte Alban guards the city of Oaxaca. In its vast plaza, we are enclosed by ancient silence. Early morning, out of tourist season, we are alone. We walk the length of the plaza, once paved, now covered by grass. There are several buildings inside the plaza, and tombs outside the confines of the structures that form the plaza's bounds. A soft wind presses against my throat. It is the breath of gods who inhabit this place as surely now as they did when there were priests to do their bidding. Cocijo, Pitao Cozobi, Quetzalcoatl, all the others.... Why, just because Time ends, would the gods leave? Gods must be invulnerable to time. Of what use are they if they are merely one more product of time? They wait. They endure. One day they will return.

At the Temple of the Dancers, I rub my hands across the distorted bodies of the Dancers. This is a temple I longed to see because dance was always a part of my life. There is some question as to whether the figures on the temple really do represent dancers or whether they might not be, instead, the inmates of a hospital, mutilated and deformed, celebrated in stone because, in ancient Mesoamerica, those with deformities were thought to possess special powers. I choose to think of the figures as dancers, able to exercise such control over their bodies that their bodies are without limits.

The advantage of not being a scholar is that one can accept any theory one chooses. One is free to make up the world as one goes along. This world made up is no less honest than the world a scholar presents. Quite possibly, because it is a more intimate world, it is more honest. In any case, it's more accessible. A scholar can describe the great civilization of Monte Alban, its meaning in 500 A.D., its decay, its artifacts, the significance of its ruins. I can describe my own civilization, its decay, the significance of its ruins.

In the distance I see my husband climbing the steps to the platform at the plaza's north end. He is as eager as I to take all this in, to absorb it, to contain it, to be contained by it. I watch him, so small against this immensity of space. Such spaces as that of Monte Alban are grand precisely so we can understand how small we are in relation to gods. I think part of why I feel the urgency I do to be in mountains is that mountains do not do this. Nature allows you your place in it. While it doesn't give you any special privileges, it does incorporate you. But this, these structures built by men to honor gods, these cannot incorporate you. They demand you remain forever apart, longing for union. Their lure is literally monumental. In the longing for union with what is sacred, there is always hope that union is possible. Without longing, there is never hope. In nature, hope is replaced by seasons. This more or less amounts to the same thing...a new chance at life. In Monte Alban, seeing my husband so small against the grandeur of those steps, these structures, this space, I feel a longing for him, for union with what is sacred. Marriage is sacred. But we do not have a marriage. In this space, I understand that. We have only longing. We came with longing and we will leave with it.

When I come upon him, he is sketching, but I think he will never paint this space.

On my last night in Oaxaca we drive into town, going, as usual, to the Zocalo. The band is playing. Girls in white dresses with long, full sweeping skirts and red sashes, their black hair braided with colored cloth, are dancing with boys in white pants, rebozos, serapes and hats. The music is too loud, too near, too insistent on dance while the dancers go through their steps without looking at one another; partners never acknowledging one another; their simple steps never leading to joy, nor to a glance or a smile. They are like the people I saw at the intersections on the day I arrived. The dance is made of dutiful, determined movement. Now here, now here, now turn, now here. The steps and the timing are perfect, but the dancers are all inside themselves.

Watching them, I understand I am leaving Oaxaca and that I have become attached to it. I have become attached to the difficulty of its life; to the hard beauty of it; to the inevitable tragic nature of the will to endure that life in it requires; to the acceptance of how life is. I would not say it, even to my husband, but I no longer want to leave.

My husband carries my suitcase down the mill stairs to the car. "I'll miss you," he says.

I see that he will, and that I will miss him, that this leaving is different than any we have yet experienced, that we will miss what we were, both of us. At the airport I wish we were leaving together. It seems too lonely to be leaving alone, even if I am on my way to adventure of my own choosing; even if, like dying and being born, there are no options here. Leaving must always be done alone.

The Warmth of a Stone Heart Lying in the Path

It is the passion of their kisses I am after, the passion of a kiss in parting. Whether the parting is one of months or years or forever, it is sealed by distance. Any kind of distance will do: miles, oceans, continents, marriages, politics, money. You have a lot of choices—about style, if not about content—when you involve yourself in partings. I know. In the ten years since that Oaxaca summer, in the years I have now lived in Montana, I've had my share of them. I've had enough, at least, to inspire a lifetime's passion. Some people might focus on the numbers of coming together those partings imply. But the beginnings lack the passion of the partings, although, as consolation, they offer hope....

When I arrived at 7:30 for Mati and Arvo's farewell party, there were a few people in the apartment—Maya, an Estonian woman living in Bozeman, and her American husband, and Lynn, a filmmaker, a woman I had often seen but never met. Mati and Arvo had come to Montana State University to take a few courses and to share with American film students their professional expertise as filmmakers in Estonia. In the months they were in Bozeman, they had built the kind of world of students and artists around them one would find in Paris or New York, a little international world of intense feeling and late night talk in a variety of languages. Their presence made Bozeman a different place.

"I caught some fish," Mati had said to me when he came to my house the night before. "You come and cook them for the party," he had said.

Light fell through the high windows of the basement apartment, and down the stairway from the open door. Granpa, the little white dog, lay curled up on the couch. Granpa had been abandoned by his owner and Mati and Arvo had adopted him, although no one had ever brushed him. Matted and dirty, he had found a home with affection. What would happen to him tomorrow, I wondered, when they left. How does a dog, so in need of love, manage when love has been there and then leaves? Mati and Arvo had named him Granpa. Perhaps he seemed ancient to them. Or wise. Or simply sad.

Fuad arrived. And Volker. And then everyone left. I was alone in the apartment. I don't know where they all went. It was one of those inexplicable things that proves everyone else knows things you don't know. I just went on preparing the fish. When everything was ready, I wandered around the apartment with Granpa following me. The living room had been cleared of all of Mati and Arvo's things. A few movie posters hung on the walls. In the bedrooms their suitcases stood ready, although these rooms looked barely touched. Books and equipment to be packed filled the shelves. Looking at all that remained to be done, it did not seem that they were leaving.

The night before, when Mati had come to visit me, he brought yellow flowers, a tape of an Estonian boys' choir, and a record of a singer, forced to leave Estonia for political reasons, who now lives in Sweden. "Our revolution was in singing," he told me. "For a month the singing went on without end." At the time it did not succeed in freeing Estonia from the Soviet Union, but perhaps God heard because, at last, Estonia is free.

Mati works in film as a sound man. His father was also a sound man. He grew up with sound, the sound of the sea and music and a paint brush moving across a canvas. For a while, between childhood and some adult time, he had been a painter. After this time in Montana, he says he will begin to paint again. When I took him and Arvo on a hike to Castle Rock, he carried sound equipment, recording as he went the sound of mountain and air, of wind through early wildflowers and across rock, of Squaw Creek rushing high and brown and fast—although it was still two weeks before flood level—the sounds of birds in trees and grouse in the underbrush, the scamperings of squirrels, the bending of grass.

Arvo photographed everything in sight, every tree and rock and instant of eternity. He would keep it all, every image that had come to him in Montana. He looked everywhere. He saw everything. Filmmaker, each image is, for him, story. "It is a simple story," he says about the film he showed me. "The Observer." A young scientist comes to a remote nature preserve where he is under the jurisdiction of a woman who is the warden. He lives in her house. He endures her anger, her bitter loneliness, her resignation. He brings her love and life and hope and in the end he leaves. To ward off poachers, self-firing rifles have been set up about the preserve. As he walks through the forest, he trips one off and he dies. She finds him and he is dead. He has left her and he is dead.

It is a wild place in which this happens, a cold, northern place of rock and water and birds, a place of great beauty without solace for the bitter, the angry, the alone.

We stood in the kitchen, Mati and I. My dog and a friend's dog lay nearby. "We have everything," Mati said. "We have dogs and a kitchen and everything we need." And later he said, "Why are you not happy? You must be happy and write books and love."

I wondered how he could see so much when our conversations were limited because his English was so sparse. Or, perhaps, ultimately, language interferes with understanding. Perhaps it is because we barely share a language that he can see what my heart screams to me all the time now. So aware of sound, perhaps he can hear the screaming of a heart.

A few more people arrived before Arvo and Mati and Fuad returned. I put the potatoes on to boil, melted butter to saute the trout. Then the room was full. People were drinking wine and vodka and dancing and Susan was telling me that she had left her husband. Susan and Arvo and Mati and another—Timothy—who was away, had formed a production company to make films. In two weeks, with no money, they had made a film about Susan, a Crow Indian, and her art. It is an art based on dreams, dreams that come out of her own traditions. They had captured, in this short film, the intensity of her connection to her tradition, to art and to humanity. No one who saw the film could believe it could have been done in less than six months.

We dream in spite of our eyes, but we cannot paint without them. Two years earlier, while Susan had been filling her car with gasoline, her eyes and face had been sprayed with gasoline when the pump suddenly erupted. Her children ran into the station for help but no one would help her, other than telling her where the ladies room was. Her daughter led her to the ladies room where she managed to splash water over her eyes, then somehow got a call through to her husband who came and took her to the emergency room. As she told me the story, we both knew that if it had been me, the station attendant would have done something to help. But she was Indian.

Her eyes. Her art. The attendant would have mattered to her, but she did not matter to him. That evening she came to a party at my house. Her eyes still burned, but she was all right. She was dressed in black and was very beautiful with her black hair and her dark eyes that did not show the pain they had suffered, but showed the depths of centuries and the knowledge of a people who have endured.

Last weekend, at a gathering with Northern Cheyenne religious leader Bill Tallbull, Tallbull's assistant, who is white, a liaison between the Indians and a white world, said to me that she thought the Indians and the Jews are a lot alike. Both have been dismissed from their own land. Both have endured its loss. I have heard Jews say the American Indian is the lost tenth tribe of Israel. Perhaps shared sorrow at the loss of land—however hidden from the self the sorrow lies—is reason enough to claim relationship.

Days after that party, a sculptor who was there said, "and there was that woman dressed in black for death." But she was dressed in the black that holds all colors and all light so deeply within itself that what we see is the soft, eternal safety of the night.

Now, at the farewell party for Mati and Arvo, Susan and I arranged the fish and potatoes on the table already laden with food and wine. "I will make a sculpture that is like falling stars," she told me, as we helped ourselves to food.

Soft night. Falling stars. Outside it had been dark for a long time. The others in the room would stay for hours more, but it was time for me to go. Mati took the box of implements and bowls I had brought out to the car and Arvo walked me up the stairs. He embraced me, holding me in the power of his will and the great strength of his arms. "You must write stories. You are so intense, it will be hard, but you must do it. The difficulty will be part of the stories."

Arvo has a wife and child in Tallinn, yet there is a way in which he can love me through a work we both understand. We connect in that place where our separate intensities feel the world, comprehending what they can, in sorrow, in joy, and—always—in observation. Understanding I needed connection to him, he understood as well that how we observed was the connection. We held one another and kissed each other's faces and then he found my mouth and pressed his own against it with the power that removes all words and the passion that removes all thought and afterward, shaking with the force of it, I knew he had been breathing life into my heart.

I found Mati near the car. He, too, had a wife waiting in Tallinn. In the light rain that began as we stood there, he held me in his arms. "Be happy," he said. "Write to me. I will practice my English."

"Last night I was happy and sad at once," he said. He kissed my forehead as lightly as the rain, and my lips with the insistence of thunder.

I was grateful for the rain as I drove home. Heaven, at least, had the grace to cry. I did not cry. I got into bed with a cup of tea and sat there and did not think. In the morning I happened to look at the clock in the kitchen at the exact moment of their departure from the airport. Then I took the dogs for a walk.

A heart-shaped stone lay in my path. "Follow the path with heart," Castaneda says. I often see heart-shaped stones, note their presence in my path and walk on. I picked this one up. It had been lying in the sun and was warm in the palm of my hand. I held it there and the warmth stayed. I heard the sound of a chain saw from somewhere down the street. I could smell the newly sawed wood. I put the warm heart in my pocket and went home.

The Train

The train was in the station when we got there, its row of cars stretching back from the soot-black engine, the cars filled with soldiers leaning out of windows. The soldiers must have been talking to people on the platform, sweethearts and parents and sisters, although I don't remember anyone on the platform but us. It is as if we alone had come to say goodbye, as if only my father had connection to this place he was leaving.

The picture of the train platform is as vivid to me as the door to the house in which I now live. I can see so clearly the broad grey platform, the train quiet and still at its edge, my father in his army uniform climbing aboard the train, blowing kisses to me. (It never occurred to me, until this moment, that he was also blowing kisses to my mother.) He waved from the steps as he boarded the train, then disappeared into the car's interior to, suddenly, reappear at a window. From the window he threw candy to me. (This, I am still sure, was meant only for me.) I was as delighted by his magical reappearance as I was by the candy flying out the window. The whole event seemed to me quite fine.

It was World War II, but all I knew about war was that

it required we all go to the train station and that my father get on the train and throw candy to me through the window. I don't know if I missed him. I do not remember him at home. I only remember going to the station. I remember him leaving.

I hardly noticed the engine at first, beyond its being attached to the cars where the soldiers were, but when it started belching smoke and screaming its whistle and the sound filled the station, the world, my head, my body, I saw how huge it was. How black. The shiny bands running from wheel to wheel began moving up and down and around in circles pressing eternally forward and the whole huge blackness of this noisy, dirty monster struggled into movement. My father's departure became swathed in smoke, filled with the screaming whistle. Terrified, I cried. I remember crying. I remember my terror. I remember my mother holding me tighter and telling me it wouldn't hurt me, my father throwing candy more furiously out the window, waving, calling goodbye over the immensity of sound as if he believed his voice could drown it out. But I could not hear his voice. The train began its heavy pull, the engine, the coal-car, then one by one the cars jolting forward until my father's car was pulled along with the rest and he leaned farther out the window waving while his car, and then the cars behind him, left the station.

Until that moment I had never experienced being left, although I suppose all children have some concept of it. Certainly, my parents must sometimes have gone out without me, but they would have left me with Mary, the black woman who took care of us all, who was as much a part of my life as my parents were, who had been present in my life as long as they had. Probably I just never noticed their going out.

Because my father, a captain in the 137th Infantry,

posted at Camp Upton, Long Island, was only about a day's train ride from where we lived, he was able to return home from time to time. At Camp Upton his job was to train troops headed for Europe and to ride a horse wherever, by that time in the U.S. Army, riding a horse was necessary. It was all ceremony then. For him, superb horseman that he was, it was the wrong war. We saw him off many times before the army finally scheduled him for shipment to Greenland, discovered he had high blood pressure and, against his will, discharged him.

My mother says that after the first time she took me to the station, they always brought someone along to carry me inside before the train left; someone to take me away from it, to allow my mother her own parting from my father. I don't remember that. I don't remember anyone but my parents. I don't really remember anyone but my handsome father in his uniform, throwing candy to me, throwing kisses, waving, leaving on the train. But, of course, if my mother is right, I only saw him leave once. All the other times, when we went to the station, it was I who left.

I suppose one parting is all one needs to understand what parting is. I suppose that ever since I watched my father leaving, after the huge, screaming blackness of his leaving, there could never be another parting, never another terror so big. Perhaps, in some kind of way, since then, it has always been me who has left. Perhaps, after the first time, that is the only parting there is. One's own. My own. Yet, what would have happened if I had finally stayed to see the empty tracks, to hear the silence in the train's wake?

Oaxaca

As I breakfasted in the garden of the house in Oaxaca, the red bougainvillea grew more and more brilliant against the walls in the early sun. The orange tree hung heavy with fruit, its fruit too bitter to eat. There was a slight breeze, the twittering of birds, the sound of gunshots in some distance. The gunshots ended. I heard them as I heard the birds, as I saw the heavy limbs of the orange tree and the brilliance of the bougainvillea. They were all a part of this garden where I sat, yet all were outside me, as a dream is outside the dreamer, as if I sat in an isolation so complete that nothing could get inside.

The bougainvillea, the birds, the gunshots, the orange tree—in the beauty of Mexico, and its violence, all of it at once, it becomes clear that moderation is a northern thought. Mexico is probably a metaphor for the human soul.

It was something I would have liked to talk about with Roberto, if only I had had the language to do it. I expected Roberto—an archeology student, a Zapotec Indian, my husband's lover—to visit later. My husband's ex-lover, that is, although they had retained a sort of friendship. My husband had returned to New York several days earlier, leaving me with the house he had rented in the city of Oaxaca, and the necessity of finding my own way in this place I had only shared with him. Although we had been apart since the summer, he asked me to come to Oaxaca to talk. He wanted to tell me that he wanted to leave Oaxaca. It seemed easier to him to talk to me there than in New York. He had a newer lover now, one who spoke English, and he had gone to New York to be with him.

Before he left, we had run into Roberto on the street. Later my husband said to me, "Roberto says your soul is great, that it comes through so clearly." I believed Roberto. Maybe I believed him because he is Indian, because he has spent centuries connected to the earth, or maybe because he, like me, is alienated from the life that seems rightfully his.

When he arrived we sat inside, at the table facing the garden. I tried to talk. He tried to help. My Spanish was too poor for us to have an entirely common language, so we spoke simply. Speaking simply leaves out the possibility of anything extra. People who talk too much should probably live in a language foreign to them for a while.

"*La vida es difícil,*" Roberto said.

"Is Oaxaca difficult for you?" I asked.

"I have friends," he said. "Friends from work, from school, but, you know, I am alone. *Me siento desconsolado. Me siento desconsolado,*" he said, his hand, one hand covering both eyes, his mouth smiling in the words he said, so that it was some time before I understood that he was crying. "*Me siento desconsolado,*" he said, over and over.

I wanted to reach for his hand, the hand lying on the table, but I was afraid he would not welcome the touch of a woman. I should have reached for his hand. He would have understood. In that moment, I was afraid there was a difference between us. I got up and brought him a box of kleenex instead.

"*Gracias,*" he said. "*Me siento desconsolado.*"

"*Las lagrimas son buenas tambien,*" I said. How useless my words seemed. I think they would have been useless in any language. How can you say, in any language, I understand your aloneness. I understand there is no end to it. You are not like anybody else. You never can be. You are alone, forever exiled from all that is simple, all that is ordinary, all that is—for other people—natural. You will find lovers. You will have work. You will never have a home—that place where there is ease, the illusion of safety. Beautiful Indian, we are alike. I think you cannot say that to someone who is alone unless you know without question that he is completely without hope.

We tried again to talk. I asked him about school. He told me he planned to return to Veracruz to get his degree, then go on for a master's and doctorate.

"I want to specialize in primitive religions," he said. "These around me are not interesting, not true—Catholicism, Protestantism, all the rest of modern religions."

"Religions of nature," I said. "Of the earth."

"Yes."

"But there are places where they still exist."

"Yes," he said. "Here, in Mexico—the Zapotec, Mixtec, they have never become Catholic. It was laid over them. They go to the church. But they are not Catholic. In their spirit, they cannot be."

"You're in a unique position for your field," I said. "You'll be important to it because of how you understand."

He shrugged. His mind connects him to his history

as fully as does his soul, this Zapotec my husband had loved. His education removes him from his people. Is it possible to study the people who you are and be them at the same time? He believes his sexuality removes him from his people. He knows his longing removes him. He cannot believe that things are possible for him, that he has a way out—or in. His dark face is grave, the deep black of his eyes ancient. There is the faintest trace of a moustache under his slightly aquiline nose. Black hair frames the sculpture, the perfect beauty, of his face.

"*Yo quiero hablar contigo,*" I said.

"*Yo tambien.*"

"I will return to Oaxaca, but learn Spanish first," I said.

"And I English."

"Your spirit is important to me," I said, annoyed at not having the words to say what I meant: I feel your soul and I value it.

"We have a communication of the spirit," he said.

"Yes, that's what I wanted to say."

When he left I gave him the three red lilies on the table. I had picked them just before he came.

"*Me siento desconsolado,*" he said again at the door.

Your tears were precious to me, Roberto, a gift. If only I could have touched them. If only I had taken your hand. Now I look for you on the street. I walked into the center of town at dusk looking for you, so certain you would appear.

There is a café on the Zocalo where I spent much of my time in Oaxaca. On this evening, as I waited there for friends, a man rode by on a horse. A boy sat behind him. A small boy crouched on the cobbles of the street between the café and the park, crying. The cathedral bells rang. Tourists thronged the park, waiting for the

Partings

mariachi band to play, examining the venders' wares—cheap, uninteresting things from Guatemala. The band played a song and then stopped. After a while, it played another song. Waiting for my friends, I thought only of Roberto who never came to that part of the Zocalo. Waiting, I watched the eyes of Indians who passed. Their eyes are like mine, only dark.

Blue

The cliff crowns the tree-covered mountain like a castle. High vertical rock towering two thousand feet above the dirt road that offers approach to it, it is an eyrie fit for gods. Or falcons.

The narrow dirt road follows a creek running cold and dark, riffling, rippling, arching and sparkling the miles of its run down from the mountains into the river in the main canyon. But on the castled mountain there is no water. There are trees and rock, grasses, shrubbery, wildflowers, mule deer, lions, mice, martens, birds. But no water. From every viewpoint on the mountain you can see the water—teasing, rushing all those feet below.

For a falcon, the flight from the cliff to the creek is no big deal. This is one of those places on earth where a falcon has all it needs—a high rock cliff safe from predators on the ground, good hunting, nearby water. The falcon's eye is powerful enough to see, from the cliff, all that is happening on the creek.

The area is one used by the Peregrine Fund for reintroduction of the once almost-extinct peregrine falcon to the wild. These sites exist across the country, on rock cliffs, on man-made towers where the situation is ideal

Partings

except for the lack of a suitable cliff, in cities. Cities being, after all, just man-made cliffs, the sheer sides of their high buildings offering the same kind of protection a peregrine falcon looks for in the wild. Some people say there are unbridgeable differences between cities and wilderness, but some people find unbridgeable differences in everything.

Environments that can support peregrines have a connection to one another, and if we cannot see the wildness for the civilization, it is only our loss. Wildness doesn't care. Wildness can take over at any moment. And it will. If we succeed in destroying life on this planet, it is wildness that will, in time, come back. Not us. The next time around life will probably try some form that works better.

Once, driving down the West Side Highway when I still lived in New York, I saw a peregrine perched on a guardrail post at about 100th Street. The falcon sat there, watching, its body perfectly still, its eyes watching. I couldn't stop on the highway. I had to drive on past, as if passing a peregrine on the West Side Highway were ordinary, something you'd do any day. At first I thought I had invented the peregrine. Later, I remembered reading about a nesting pair under the George Washington Bridge. The George Washington Bridge connects New York to New Jersey and the Rocky Mountains. For a number of years I had been driving up the highway from my apartment on the Upper West Side, across the bridge, then straight west to Wyoming or Montana. The bridge was a direct link between my house and the Rocky Mountains.

In the first summer after I moved permanently to Montana, I went to work for the Peregrine Fund as a hack site attendant, one of two people assigned to each peregrine release site in the country, to feed, observe, track and generally watch out for the young peregrines hatched in the laboratory, but hacked to the wild. Hacking is a falconer's term for a process that allows for the natural physical conditioning of birds of prey taken from the nest before they can fly. The falconer places the young bird on some conspicuous structure (the Peregrine Fund uses a wooden box that becomes the birds' home until they are old enough to begin flying) and provides them with food. Once the birds start flying they still return daily to the site for food. As they learn to hunt and begin making their own kills, they spend more and more time away from the hack site. At this point the falconer retraps the birds and tames them to be trained for sport. The Peregrine Fund, on the other hand, simply prays they have learned enough to survive in the wild. Eighty percent of them do not.

Three days before I was to begin my eight weeks as an attendant, I had a climbing accident that resulted in my right arm requiring six stitches and an unstitchable hole in my right leg below my knee. I could put little pressure on my leg and could hardly use my arm. I am right-handed. I had to drive in second gear because my left arm could not reach far enough to push the shift into any higher gear. The job required a daily climb of about sixty feet down to the ledge where the young peregrines were kept in their hack box, as well as tending to camp chores.

Why had I done this just before the beginning? I had been looking forward to this time on the mountain for months. It had been the only thing besides the move to Montana I had been able to focus on fully since my marriage of eighteen years had broken up. Had I deliberately sabotaged it? I believe there are no accidents.

Partings

Coincidence does not exist. Things that seem random are merely unfathomable. Would I have to cancel? How could I at this point? I phoned the Peregrine Fund to let them know what had happened. "Can you get up to camp?" the director asked me. "Yes," I answered. "Your partner can take care of the climbing." He was calming, reassuring. It all seemed possible, yet I was devastated. My partner would be up there with the birds, while I would be in camp, watching through the spotting scope.

I arrived at the meeting spot on time, Thursday at noon. One of two biologists who would help us set up camp arrived soon after. The other, coming from Boise, Idaho with my partner and our falcons, arrived two hours late. They had been on the road since one in the morning. My partner, Stefania, looked dazed and disheveled from the long trip. When she lifted her backpack onto her back for the first haul up to camp, the sleeping bag, awkwardly tied at the bottom, dangled half off the pack. The backpack itself was army surplus. This woman would take care of the climbing?

Leaving our backpacks at the campsite, we followed the biologists who carried four baby falcons in two large square cardboard cartons boxes marked "Hertz Rent-All" up to the cliff where the hack box sat on a narrow ledge, tethered to the ledge by cables nailed into the rock behind the box. There was just room at the sides of the box and in front for a person to stand. The biologists showed Stefania, who had never climbed before, how to use her climbing harness and how to tie into the belay set up around a sturdy tree at the top of the climb. Then all three downclimbed the cliff that led to the ledge, and hiked across the ledge to prepare the hack box. I watched them go down and across and work at the box, wretched because I had allowed myself to be left out.

They had taken one carton of falcons with them. While they were occupied at the hack box, I peeked through one of the airholes in the remaining carton, and came eye to eye with a falcon. I was not supposed to do this, not supposed to disturb the baby birds in any way, disturb them any more than they had already been disturbed by being taken from the only place they had ever known, put into a box and driven some four hundred miles through the night to be carried up two thousand feet and a mile and a half of mountain. I knew I wasn't supposed to. At the peephole, a great, round, dark, fierce eye drew my own eye in.

When the hack box was ready, the biologists returned for the remaining falcons. At the box again, the three of them watched as the falcons settled into their new home. It seemed a long time that I watched the biologists and Stefania observing the birds. When the biologists felt sure everything was in order, the three walked back across the ledge and climbed up the wall. We packed the climbing gear into a stuff bag, tied it to the tree where it would stay for the duration, and hiked back down to camp. The hot sky clouded over. It was almost 7:00 when we reached camp.

We still had a few loads waiting to be carried up to camp, and camp to be set up. One of the biologists, the only male among us, began hauling 80-pound containers of water the thousand feet, three-quarter mile climb from the road to camp. There was no water at the campsite. Every drop we used had to be carried up. I would have to keep my wounds clean without water. What we had was too precious for that and needed for drinking and cooking. Rain began as we put up the tent. Hurrying, we threw our gear into it, then headed back to the road for the final load. It was late now, and growing dark. The last ascent to camp would be in darkness.

Stefania, who I had already seen was very strong, and a faster walker than I am even when my leg is all right, was afraid there would be bears in the dark. On this return, I went first, grateful for the night, for the end of this day. Observer. My usual role. It's why I'm a writer. But I am an actor as well, and on this day I was out of the essential action. I had become too much what I already was.

I walked without using my flashlight, feeling the path more than seeing it. The rain stopped. The night cleared. Starlight reflected off white stones. Earth and sky were the same. My feet were on earth, my head in sky. I liked walking in the night. Besides, I knew there were no bears. Confiding my one anxiety about this site to a landscape architect I knew who worked for the national forest where the site was located, I had said, "The only thing I'm worried about is bears."

"There ain't no fuckin' bears up there," she reassured me.

At camp we got the stove going, ate a late dinner and had a chance, finally, to meet one another.

Stefania had been hired the day before. When the Peregrine Fund had told me that my partner could take care of the climbing, I actually had no partner. My original partner had called them the day before I called to say she'd taken a job training horses in Colorado. The director had sounded so calm. He must have been frantic, but he also must have had faith this would work out. Climber, falconer, he has spent a lifetime being patient.

I'd hardly thought about my partner beforehand. You would think that someone about to spend eight weeks living in a tent with another person with whom they would be together more or less twenty-four hours a day might spend a little time wondering about that person. It is, after all, the kind of time that could cement a love affair or a friendship forever, or end either one in a short time. Taking on that kind of time with a stranger is a bit like answering an ad for a mail-order bride, except this one had fewer outs.

But I'd only thought about the falcons. After the accident, I just hoped she or he would be competent, but I worried that terrific competence would make me extraneous. I did not want to be extraneous. I wished I was doing this alone. I wished I hadn't injured myself.

Stefania was a volunteer at the World Center for Birds of Prey in Boise—Peregrine Fund headquarters— and a recent zoology graduate. When my erstwhile partner called to say she'd taken another job, and I called to say I couldn't climb, the Peregrine Fund asked Stefania if she was free to take this on. They asked her late in the afternoon of the day before we were to open the site. She had a job commitment for that evening, so it was 11:00 at night before she began getting her gear together. Not that she had much. She had been backpacking one weekend in her life. Somehow she managed to borrow a pack and sleeping bag, throw together a few clothes, and take off at one in the morning with the biologist who was bringing the birds. She had slept a little in the truck, but not much.

She hauled gear up from the vehicles parked on the road below. She climbed easily down to the hack box. She climbed a tree near camp to tie the rope from which we would suspend our food coolers. (Food must be suspended from trees in Montana—to keep it out of reach of ground squirrels as much as bears.) She dug the latrine. She helped me get the tent up and arrange a tarp to shelter our kitchen. I apologized that I could do so little, but she handled everything with grace. She asked how to do the things she had never done, then did them simply, without making me feel how little I could actually do. She was physically strong, and incredibly gentle in her relation to me, to all that was around us, work and birds and earth and heaven.

She was twenty years younger than I, and we would become friends.

For the first couple of mornings, we hiked up to the cliff together. Then she climbed down to leave the quail we had brought for the falcons to eat, watched the falcons through peepholes in the box and climbed back up while I sat on top of the cliff, pistol in hand—to shoot blanks at any passing eagles and scare them out of the territory before they got the idea there were young peregrines here to harass. We did not want them around once the peregrines were out of the box. On the rocks above the cliff, watching the sky, I felt sick with longing for connection with the birds. I knew I had to climb.

The doctor had told me the one thing I must guard against was banging either wound, or I risked serious infection, no trifle under field conditions. But a friend, Bob, a strong man, was coming to camp on Saturday. I decided to go down to the box while he was there. If I had problems at all with the climb, he was strong enough to simply haul me up again.

My knees felt shaky as I stepped into my climbing harness. Bob stood at the top of the cliff, waiting for me to start. I started slowly, reaching with my foot down the narrow wall for the little knob that would allow me a beginning. I was frightened, but I had started. The knob was solid, easy. And the next and the next. It was not hard. On the rock I saw it was not hard. A vertical staircase. When I looked up I could see Bob standing calmly at the top, Stefania behind him. I was still nervous, but it was easier now, having started, than it had been standing on top, thinking about it. Doing a thing is easier than not doing it. And there was Bob. I could see him, leaning over the edge until I reached the very bottom where view of him was cut off by the wall itself. But then I didn't need to see him anymore. I had done it. I had only to walk across the ledge to the birds. I untied and made my way to the hack box. Here now for the reason I had come, I was no longer separate. I lifted the flap on one of the peepholes, keeping my finger over the hole until my eye covered it so that, for the birds, the dark wall would remain uninterrupted.

Four peregrines stood there looking out the front of the box at swallows and insects flitting past, at bits of down from their own coats that floated out on the light, bright sky forming their view of the world. Babies. Grave, funny birds with down sprouting out from under their wings and sticking through their breast feathers. I could already see how different each was from the others. We had decided against naming them because, in the wild, peregrines do not have names, and because names could engender attachment on our part, attachment in some more personal way than the kind of universal attachment to all of life. We were there to observe and record, not to love. But it was still necessary for us to identify them individually. We decided to refer to them by the color of the leg bands the Peregrine Fund had attached to their right legs to identify them. On their left legs they wore black federal bands with a number given each by the U.S. Department of Fish & Wildlife. The result was that the words blue, yellow, red and green became as much names for us as Richard or Chloe.

Partings

From the front of the box, the peregrines' view was of sky, of forest below the sky, forest falling away to the creek, of forest and mountains beyond the creek reaching up to sky again. Everything there was was defined by sky.

The peregrines watched everything that passed and took considerable note of each other's movements. They preened, spread their wings, moved about the box, jumping on and off the two rock perches on the box floor. Each bird was different from the others, but one was more different. Blue. Boldest, most regal, he was the most active of the four. He spread his wings with such air of majesty that you knew you were in the presence of no ordinary bird. He jumped from one rock perch to the other, jumped at the bars, at the box door. He jumped on the other peregrines. The box seemed too small for him. He was so eager for the world. Blue was beautiful. They were all beautiful, but Blue was the most beautiful. Wild, wild and beautiful.

Soon after they were released from the box, eight days after they arrived, Blue jumped to the top of the box to check out the world. He was the second to fly, but he flew as if he understood flight from the moment of birth. The other falcons, like most falcons, made short flights in the beginning, practice flights, learning what flight is, how to take off and to land, their practice strengthening the muscles needed for longer forays. Blue didn't bother with all that. He took off in a bee-line for the ridge to the east, flew behind it, and was gone.

He was really gone. He did not come back that day to eat, nor the next, nor the next. We had been told a young falcon could survive four days without food. That is, if it didn't encounter an owl or a golden eagle, or didn't land on the forest floor from which it might have a hard time launching itself skyward again. On the forest floor a young falcon was easy prey for foxes or lynx, coyotes, badgers. In the air it could be taken down by other raptors. It is a favorite food of owls. More than once has a young falcon's radio transmitter been found lying at the foot of an owl's tree, tangled among a few cleaned bones. Just out of the box, the falcon doesn't know how to hunt, does not have the skill to out-maneuver a predator in flight, has no technique for evasion, or the security of that tremendous power into which it will grow. The first weeks for a young falcon are treacherous ones.

We searched for Blue with the telemetry, picking up his signal in one direction and, almost immediately, in the opposite direction. It came weakly from what seemed great distances, or it bounced along ridges, reflecting back from them. We hiked miles trying to pick up a clear direction, imagining—against our wills—that the weak signal came from the transmitter lying at the foot of some owl's tree. By the third day we were pretending calmness. By the fourth, we believed he must be dead. He was a baby. What skill could he have to survive so long on his own?

I searched the sky for him and he did not return. In spite of the other three in the sky, the sky seemed empty to me. As empty as the house seems, or the town, when one's lover is absent. No, lover is the wrong word. Beloved. The one who makes the world exist on that plane where everything is seen, felt, experienced in full clarity of its power, its grace, its unutterable beauty, its hope and its amazing life. Some magic, glorious, soaring moment had disappeared from me. The more I mourned his loss, the more he became, for me, mine. I continued to watch the others, to note their every action in my notebook. I was fascinated by them, but I felt empty. My peregrine was gone....

Partings

I am not the first woman to fall in love with a bird. There was Leda, for instance. Even if her swan wasn't a real bird, but just a god, she thought it was a bird. In love, imagination is everything.

In the late afternoon of the fifth day Stefania and I were both sitting at the scopes in the meadow. It had been a hot day. The birds had spent the heat of the afternoon roosting in cool niches on the wall. Now, with the sun lower, they erupted into the sky. Watching them shoot up from the wall, I suddenly realized there were four peregrines in the sky.

Blue had come back. Blue was alive. My beautiful bird was alive. He had gone far and come back and he was alive. He flew with the others, the four of them filling the sky with the glory of falcons and the miracle of return. Blue had come back.

Our days settled into routine. We alternated mornings to climb up to the box and leave the day's allotment of quail, each of us making the thousand foot, three-quarter mile climb to the cliffs alone, tying in, climbing down. I was nervous about that at first, but, as the days went on I grew calmer, realizing I knew what I was doing, and needed only be willing to trust that I knew. I relished that morning time. I felt as if the peregrines were mine alone. I could climb. I was strong. I was healthy. I was healing.

I was happier than I had ever been. I began to see my fall as a gift, a chance to see what healing is. Why, after all, did nothing break when I landed so hard, and in so complicated a way, on rock? How was it that I was able to walk away from the fall, to get to the hacksite on time?

I had received two difficult and serious wounds, but they were wounds that would heal, that I could watch healing. They required enormous attention (an hour a day was spent, under none too clean "field" conditions), but they were healing. Healing takes time and leaves scars, but it makes one whole. The process was identical to that my psyche and soul had been undergoing since the end of my marriage. The gift I was given was the chance to see how the process works. I don't know if it is possible to understand more by watching the process, but it is possible to see the process happen; to feel the relief and joy of healing; the good luck of it; to feel how resilient one is after all; how whole one can become.

It happens in its own time. It is in the course of things.

So is the sunrise and the day and the sunset, the easy comfort Stefania and I developed with one another—a balance no different from the balance of meadow grass and forest, and the glorious flight of peregrines erupting into the sky, soaring, diving, flipping over, turning so that the sun glints off their breasts, chasing one another and tumbling through the sky like puppies on the ground, falling free to rise again on some splendid moment of air.

How near, how intimate the sky becomes.

Toward the end of August the air smelled of autumn. It happened overnight. The mornings became cool and I built fires to warm us during breakfast, then sat over coffee in front of the fire, watching the cliff. The birds were learning to hunt, although it was still a game for them. We continued setting out quail, but cut back to every other day shortly before closing the site in September. The peregrines would leave soon. Picking up their rightful instinct, they would join in with other passing raptors and be gone. This, too, is in the course of things.

After the Horse Died

We knew Johnny would die. Red. Johnny Walker Red. The Tennessee Walker with the long ears who always picked his head up to walk grandly toward people when he heard them on the path. He might prefer to be somewhere else than carrying his rider up a trail, but he would never present anything to the world but a horse of beauty and spirit, eager to be on his way. He was the first horse I rode. I climbed up on him bareback in East Glacier and Bruce led me around the yard where he was pastured for a few days during my visit. After I had ridden bareback, Bruce saddled him and showed me how to make him turn. I was as frightened of horses as I had always been, yet I was already different than I had been. Before I came to Montana I could not even reach over a fence to pet a horse, but now, here I was, on one.

One day I was at the house alone when Johnny got a rear hoof caught in the wire of the yard fence. There was nothing to do but get it out. He stood quietly while I worked at the wire. Even when he was finally free, he did not move quickly, but simply put the hoof on the ground, stood for a moment, then walked away.

Later that summer Bruce borrowed a horse for me,

Shadow, another Tennessee Walker with whom Johnny had been pastured for years, and we went into the Bob Marshall Wilderness for a few days. Johnny was always the leader, Shadow always behind. I don't remember the trails anymore, but I do remember the warmth of the horses, the pleasure of their company, the sense of connection—to animal, earth and history. I did not yet know how to saddle and bridle a horse, or how to be assertive enough to force Shadow to walk beside Johnny where the trail was wide enough, but I was no longer so frightened as I had been. I knew I would learn to ride, that horses were no longer foreign.

When I left East Glacier to return to New York to arrange for my permanent move to Montana, both Johnny and Shadow were in the yard. We loaded the car and then it was time for me to go. The horses came over to the fence next to the car. They stood there, their heads over the fence. They had come to say goodbye.

By the time I returned, Bruce had moved from East Glacier to Bozeman, bringing Johnny to the Paradise Valley, where he remained with Jeanette and Brian, the friends who had once pastured him in East Glacier. They had built a log house in the valley, in the meadows bounding a creek that came down from the Absarokas. The mountains were always there, beyond the fields, rounded and treed here, then reaching back into the depths of the range, to high peaks and dense forests out of the sight of houses and ranches, out of sight of the Yellowstone River that forms the Paradise Valley. From the house we could see the mountains and the Yellowstone River and the Gallatin Range west of the river. At night the stars came down to the mountains and the horses moved like shadows in the pasture. I liked lying in bed in that house, looking out the window as

Partings

night lightened into morning, as night, waning, absorbed stars one by one back into it, leaving a few—the brightest few—to ease the coming of day. Stars disappeared. Mountains appeared. I loved the coming of morning in that house, in that valley.

Bruce often housesat for Jeanette and Brian, commuting back and forth to Bozeman during the week. I always came out on weekends. We walked in the mountains. He rode Johnny. I even got on Johnny a few times, although I was always afraid to ride him away from the house because it took someone far more assertive than I to keep him from running back. Sometimes I brushed him. Sometimes I just went to talk to him. Sometimes I had little to do with him, as if he would always be there.

One spring I rode him around the pasture. He was amenable and quiet. Then Bruce rode him. Afterward he seemed almost lame. He was breathing hard, although he had not been ridden hard. Not long after that Jeanette called Bruce to tell him Johnny was sick. She had had the vet out and they were trying some medication, but she didn't know if it would work. No one seemed to know precisely what was wrong, although they suspected cancer. I suppose Bruce began preparing himself then, although I could not imagine that something couldn't be done. A few days later Jeanette told Bruce that the medication hadn't had much effect, but the vet was out of town and they were putting Johnny on steroids to ward off his obvious pain until the vet's return.

Even I understood then that Johnny would die. I went out one afternoon to see him. He was standing in the early summer pasture, knee deep in grass, eating. I told him I had come to say hello. I could not bring myself to say I had come to say goodbye.

Johnny had been dead a few weeks when, in mid-August, Bruce told me he was going out to housesit. "Will it be hard for you, Johnny not being there?" I asked.

"He's there," he answered.

"Will you be there for your birthday?" I asked. "I'll bring out dinner."

"I don't know what I'll do for my birthday," he said, adding, after a moment, "Tina called from Alaska a few weeks ago to say she would be passing through about the third week in August."

"But not for your birthday...."

We had spent our birthdays together since we had met, except for those few times we had been in different states. I still imagined I would go out to the Paradise Valley for his birthday.

"I'll come out...."

"I don't want you to."

He left for the valley on Monday. He called me once during the week. I made arrangements to go to the Tetons for the weekend with friends so that I would not just be sitting around my house thinking about his birthday. I asked if he would take care of my dog. We often took care of one another's dogs. Yes, he said, he would come to my house at lunchtime so the dog would know he hadn't been abandoned, then pick him up after work. When I left the house on Friday morning, the dog cried in a way I had never heard him cry. Seeing my preparations, he expected to go along. When he understood he was being left behind, he began to cry. His cries tore at me. Concerned about him, I called Bruce in the afternoon to make sure he had found the dog all right at lunchtime. "I've been too busy," he told me. "I haven't been able to stop for lunch yet." Then he added, "I told

Tina she would have to leave on Monday. Do you want to come out Monday night? They've sold the house so this will be the last time that I'm there."

"Is she really leaving?"

"I told her she had to."

"Yes," I said. "I'd like to come out. I care about that place."

In the Tetons I could not stop thinking about Bruce's birthday, and about the house in the Paradise Valley. When he picked me up after work on Monday, I could not speak to him. I could not understand what had happened. Johnny had died. The people had sold the house. A woman had come to Bruce there. When I got into his truck, I saw things of hers scattered about. "Is she in your house?" I asked.

"Yes," he answered.

"I thought you told her she had to leave."

"She was waiting for some slides to arrive that I wanted to see. I told her she could stay until Tuesday, and after that I'd give her a list of campgrounds."

"Did you sleep with her?"

"Do you want to get into that now?"

"I want to know where I am."

"Yes."

When I got out of the truck at the house, my head felt disconnected to the rest of me, light and pressed at once, dizzy. My legs seemed to have no bones in them. I wanted to strike out, to hit, to kick, to vent the rage that sucked at my heart. I hit and cried and felt myself sinking into the ground. I felt him holding me but understood he no longer held me as a lover. There was thunder, a few sprinkles of rain. After a long time Bruce said, "Johnny's grave is just over there. There probably isn't much time before the storm, if you want to visit him."

I got up then and went to the pasture where Johnny was buried. I wondered which way his head was. I sat on the ground next to the way I thought it might be. I apologized to Johnny for telling him I had come to say hello rather than goodbye. There was a stone on the grave that was almost the shape of a horse's head. It was a horse's head without the ears. Johnny's ears had been so marvelous, but this horse did not have ears. Maybe ears don't really matter. What is it, after all, that we hear? And what is it that we cannot hear? I took the stone. "Goodbye, Johnny," I said.

Poet

The main street of Yellow Springs, Ohio, is more chic than it was thirty years ago when I went to school there. But the Old Trail Tavern, where we went for burgers and 3.2 beer is still there. So is the Little Art Theatre where I sold tickets to the films—most of which I remember as French—that formed forever my views of what film should be. My boyfriend managed the theatre. He had red hair and a red beard and was handsome in a Christ-like sort of way. Until he began managing the theatre, he was a sandal maker. I haven't seen him since I left school, but someone wrote me a year ago from California, where he lives, that he looks exactly the same, except his hair and beard are snow white.

Many of Yellow Springs' houses date from the late 19th century. They look like houses in Bozeman. I never thought of Yellow Springs as a 19th century town when I went to school there, although in those days I thought the 19th century was about literature, not architecture. Now, seeing the houses, I understood why Bozeman had been so immediately familiar to me. Bozeman is bigger and possessed of an almost daily increase in its 20th century sprawl, and is surrounded by mountains to boot but, if you don't look up, the similarity seems greater than the difference.

I had come to Yellow Springs for the Antioch Writers Workshop, an annual event on the Antioch College campus. My college writing teacher and advisor, the poet Jud Jerome, was an integral part of the workshop. It was he who had invited me to attend. He figured I could be useful somewhere in it, and thought that I would find it interesting.

Although Jud and I had had no contact for most of the years since I had left Yellow Springs, we had begun a correspondence two years earlier, after I sent him a copy of a book in which I had mentioned him. The correspondence was an enormous act of grace on his part because I had made a mistake in the book.

In the book I said that, having discovered a passage in Hemingway's "A Clean, Well-Lighted Place" where the dialogue between two waiters was illogical, I had written to Hemingway and told him that and he had answered saying it was perfectly clear to him. I went on to say that I had given the letter to my teacher because he had wanted it.

That is not what happened. I had gone to Jud with the passage and told him it didn't make sense. He had looked at it and agreed and then he had written to Hemingway on college stationery, signing his name and title—"Assistant Professor of English." Months later Hemingway sent the letter back, scrawling in the margin, "Dear Assistant Professor Jerome, I just reread it and it makes sense to me. Sorry, E.H." Jud never again signed his name with his title.

The letter (of which I now have a copy) is in the Judson Jerome Collection at Boston University Library where it was examined by a professor who later published something about it, setting off a whole scholarly industry revolving around finding passages of Hemingway dialogue in which the speakers did not alternate in the expected sequence. "The literary scholars had come to the conclusion that this was a deliberate technique," Jud wrote me. "I remember writing the professor to the effect that it might be a technique, but it was a lousy technique, introducing confusion without deepening meaning."

"I assure you," he went on, "that I wasn't at all bothered by your mistake. Indeed, I had forgotten that you were the one who pointed out the problem to me. I thought I had discovered it all by myself! But it's a real problem in that passage...it doesn't make sense for sure. I was amused by what you said in your book—and realized how muddied our memories can be. I'm discovering a lot of that these days, working on the second volume of my memoirs. I think we have a rewrite button in our heads, such as the Stalinists used on history, to make it all come out all right."

I suppose it did all come out all right. We had each made a mistake, so I guess we came out even, although mine was certainly more public.

I put off accepting Jud's invitation for months because, although I was eager to see him, and curious about the school and the town and who I was when I had been there, the time of year really was wrong. Leaving Montana to go to Ohio at the beginning of July, the beginning of Montana's summer, the time I do most of the outdoor things I write about the rest of the year, seemed irresponsible to me. Not to mention dumb. The time is so brief in Montana when it is possible to get into the mountains easily. Summer is short and utterly beautiful. In Ohio it is beastly hot.

I kept thinking that perhaps the timing would be better some other year. Yet, by spring, it occurred to me that the timing of things is never any better and if I meant to do it, I should simply do it. I felt ready to connect with what was past and curious to see what new things that old time could bring. And, after his letters, it seemed essential to connect with Jud. He had been the only person who had tried to keep me in school when I decided to drop out. I had not listened to him then. Perhaps because I understood that he was right, I could not listen to him. There is a necessity, when you are young, to make serious mistakes. This allows you the rest of your life to analyze them. It allows you to never again take anything for granted; to understand the difference between choice and obsession; to see with far greater clarity than you ever imagined, your own relationship to the universe. I was ready to listen to him now.

I wrote to the workshop director and told her I would come.

A few weeks before my planned departure, a letter arrived from Jud. "Dear Correspondent," was followed by an apology for a canned letter. "I'm going through a 'closing down' phase because it is clear that cancer will have a radical effect on my life...," Jud wrote. "It has been determined that I have a fairly aggressive large cell cancer apparently stemming from a small mass in the lung inaccessible to surgery.... I've heard that there's some chance that if cancers like mine come on quickly, they may quickly be defeated. Something like half those who contract this particular variety seem to be cured by the particular 'protocol' of chemotherapy that I'm on, so 'closing down' hasn't for me, any particular sense of finality about it. This simply seems a good time, ceremoniously, to tidy up the workshop of my mind, to set some things aside, perhaps for good, to finish up some others, and, most importantly, to rededicate my energy to some new ones.... The occasion of this illness seems to me to be revving up my creative energy; it's 'fasten seatbelts' time. I feel like I'm taking off with unimaginable excitement and anticipation (never mind a little pain here and there, occasional nausea, and, it seems, stretches of lassitude)."

My instinct was to cancel the trip. If Jud would not be available, there was, I thought, no reason to go. This may not seem an appropriate response when someone writes you he has cancer, but I am sure I am not the first person to feel betrayed by someone else's cancer. Cancer. Cancel. They're almost the same word. Perhaps they are the same word, although the one thing I felt from Jud's letter was that his cancer was the opposite of cancel. His cancer was a challenge, a raging call to life. His letter was designed to keep its readers from fear or mourning, to engage them in the triumph of challenge, in an insistence on life. Once again, Jud had come through with extraordinary grace.

On the first of July, a perfect Montana summer day, I loaded my car and drove east. In Yellow Springs, I found my way to the campus easily, but once there it was as if I had never seen it before. Everything seemed foreign. Some buildings were boarded up; others looked abandoned. A few newer buildings looked cheap and dilapidated, although I suppose that if school had been in session, it would have looked different. I had no idea which was the dorm where I had lived. I had no memory of the hall where the writers' workshop was taking place, although it was obviously not a new building. I stood in line waiting to register, wondering how it was that nothing at all remained to me of those years.

An hour later I walked over to the Main Building where Jud was giving a reading as part of a program of poetry, music and dance in his honor. I did not remember the theatre in which the event was being held any more than I remembered anything else about the campus. (The next day, in the fiction workshop, the instructor began his class by saying "Remembering gets in the way of memory." What he meant is that if you can let go of reporting facts, you are free to come to the essence of feeling. I took this as a personal message....)

At Jud's reading, everyone in the audience—which seemed to consist largely of people who had graduated, then found a way to stay in Yellow Springs—looked as everyone had when I was in school; the same intense, ascetic faces; the same instincts toward peasant fabric and color in their clothes; the same rapt attention that swept from their faces down their bodies to performance, to word, to sound—only they all seemed to have grey hair. Jud was already reading when I slid into a seat on the side aisle. Hearing his voice, I remembered it. He looked as I remembered him too, the young teacher not so many years older than I, slight, intense and laughing at once. Lacking some brooding darkness, he had not looked like a poet to me then. He did now. Down there at the edge of the theatre, slight and brave and insistent on life, whatever its pain, he seemed the essence of poet to me. The difference between youth and middle age is not physical. It is in how you see the soul.

Jud's poems were reminiscences of a life intimately observed, moving and funny and wise and full of hope. When he finished his first round, a dancer from the Dayton Ballet performed. She seemed heavy, but willing. I heard later that she was well over six feet tall. She looked large, but you can't really tell how tall a person is when she or he is alone on a stage. Jud read again, his voice strong in his wonderful words. Then a chamber music ensemble performed, although they dismissed one of their pieces after a few false starts, saying they simply hadn't practiced it enough. I had to leave before the concert was over to get to my lodgings and back to campus in time for the kick-off banquet.

Jud entered the dining room as the instructors were being introduced during dessert. He sat on the far side of the room from me. When my name was called he raised his arms over his head, joining his hands and shaking them in salute, smiling with a joy that made me proud I had come. Minutes later he left the dining room looking ill.

I was told by the workshop director that he would teach the poetry class the next day, but after that would be in the hospital. She suggested I call him in the morning.

Standing before the class, Jud looked exactly as he had as my teacher. I had seen recent photos of him with a huge shock of white hair, but now, what hair he had was very close to his head, courtesy of the chemotherapy. His hair had also been very short when he was my teacher so I did not see a man who had lost his hair, but the same young teacher who had stood before class thirty years earlier. On the telephone, Jud had asked if I would drive him home after class and stay for lunch. I met him in the hall after class and he embraced me, kissing me with a powerful urgency that had nothing to do with man and woman, or old friends. It was the urgency of the present toward eternity, of the artist toward art, of life against dismissal. It was as if he would give me life, would form me like the poem to which he gives his breath and his passion. In his kiss was his own insistence on life, the urgent, eternal, absolute necessity of life—there, in his kiss, was all there is of life.

"You are more beautiful than you were," he said. I smiled at him. "We're all more beautiful, aren't we..." he said.

It was true. All of us are. "Yes," I said. "We are."

At lunch, Jud and Maggie—a New York magazine editor who had been his student a few years before me and who had been close to Jud and his family ever since—and I ate sandwiches in a room lined with books and talked about Hemingway, laughing over the to-do evolving from the question about which waiter was talking. Then Jud read to us, a long poem recently published in a small magazine. The poem struck both Maggie and me as marvelously funny and we laughed throughout Jud's reading. Even he paused occasionally to smile. It was a poem about a man who has always done everything in exactly the same way but who suddenly finds himself on an unfamiliar road on his way home from work. The road leads him into places of dark dreams, yet, rather than a sense of nightmare, we felt adventure, the irreversible and inevitable inexplicable in a life of routine.

We both saw the poem almost more than we heard it, it was so completely visual. I asked the two screenwriters who were conducting the screenwriting classes if they would read it—something I would normally never do, but this, after all, was for Jud. Besides, I felt so sure. When they gave the copies back to me, they each said (sadly—they wanted me to be right about it) it was not a film, not visual at all, not a story to be filmed, not, in fact, the least bit funny, as I had told them it was. What they saw was the darkness.

"But we laughed the whole time Jud was reading," I said.

"That's the art of a performer," they said.

When it was time for us to go, Jud walked Maggie and me out to the car. He would be going into the hospital the next day. He knew it would make him sick, but he believed it would also make him well. "I'm going to beat this thing," he said to me. I believed him.

Several days later, on an impulse as I walked past the Yellow Springs post office, I decided to buy stamps in case I had time to write a few postcards. I was not aware of having been in the post office before, and it certainly was not someplace I thought about, but the instant I walked inside, I knew—for the first time in the days I had been in Yellow Springs—where I was. Nothing at all about it was changed. No time had passed. I was not there now, but then. All that has happened was yet to come. The force of the memory was enormous. Or, rather, it was not memory at all. The actual place may be a catalyst to memory, but it is not memory. It is some unexpected moment of touching home base so you can go on from there.

What is curious is the form home base takes. I am sure it is never the form one seeks. The act of seeking automatically changes the thing sought. The thing you find by chance is something you had never considered. The campus had changed, the town had changed, Jud had changed, I had changed. The post office had remained the same.

A post office is an odd reference point although, in some small eastern Montana farm towns where everything—even the saloon and cafe—has closed down, the post office is the one public place still functioning. People meet in post offices all over the country. It is a crossroad, the junction where communication passes en route from one place to another. Sometimes the communication gets lost, held up, torn up in the machinery. Sometimes it is delivered in record time. In any case, it is words that pass through a post office. It is connection. And, I had come because of Jud's letters....

Two months later, when I was back in Montana, and Maggie in New York, I was talking to her on the phone. She told me that Jud's brother and another old friend were visiting him a month after the workshop when Jud asked his doctor, "Am I going to die?"

"Yes," the doctor answered.

"Then I want some really good whisky," Jud said.

"Go for it," the doctor said.

Maggie said Jud's wife went out and got the best whisky she could find. The three men spent the night drinking that good whisky and talking. The next day Jud died.

Winter

The warm, moist Florida air hits you full force as you exit the West Palm Beach terminal. It wraps you like a blanket. It is an air that encloses you, as a room encloses you, its walls cutting off access to the world beyond. It is a heavy air in which you must stay as still as possible, a prisoner in the room, although the room expands to include the highway with its six lanes of high speed bumper-to-bumper traffic, the vehicles like dust motes dancing on a ray of light falling into the room. It includes huge complexes of uniform houses and apartment buildings creeping over every inch of visible land as if Florida's native growth was white stucco. It includes rows of car rental agencies, chain restaurants, furniture stores, malls. I have never driven the length of the room, but I suppose it must extend south to the Everglades and north the whole way of the coast. How neatly developers have dispensed with the chaos of nature, the wild tangles of mangrove, the coniferous forests, the swamps and grasslands that once covered this tropical wetland in greens of dense mystery and humid silence.

My brother picked me up at the airport in the car my father, who no longer drives, gave to him. My brother has involved himself in local politics, suddenly becoming an activist fighting to retain a not very large open green space on the Intercoastal Waterway. There are few left in this part of Florida. This one will probably not be left much longer since a developer managed his way around the laws of the town in which the green space sits to finagle the go-ahead for a huge development on the land. My brother is angry at the thought of the loss of the land. He is also angry that the town will not use its laws to stand up to the developer, but that it, like virtually every other town in America, is perfectly willing to sacrifice almost anything to someone with money. Although it is probably possible to show that the cost to the taxpayer as open space is far less than the cost to the taxpayer as a development, the reporter from the Palm Beach Post who attended a town meeting in which a petition signed by about 1500 people opposing the development was presented, intimated in his article the next morning that the petitioners were obstructionists who would be dealt with.

One day my brother and I rode in his old Chris Craft up the Intercoastal Waterway. Except for that one green space, fronted by mangroves dipping into the water, the miles we covered were lined with enormous houses whose perfect lawns sloped down to the Intercoastal where large boats were moored, and with apartment complexes that must have gotten slid in there while the owners of the huge houses weren't looking. In the green space, the mangroves seemed a transition between water and earth. Their twisting roots rise from the edge of earth and water in mazes of arches that return to the edge, a kind of immediate announcement that air, earth and water are all necessary for life. Inside the green space, blocked from our view by the tangle of vegetation at the water's edge, there are climbing shrubs, a jungle of trees, the choking profusion of damp, green life. Raccoons live there, opossum, foxes, otters, muskrats, squirrels, birds. As we passed by, a heron fished at the edge of the mangroves. A coolness flowed out of the green space toward us, wafting across the calm water of the Intercoastal. It was like passing a cave in the mountains whose entranceway offers its own eternal air, a private climate, a freshness unsullied by the world outside the cave. The cave offers shelter, mystery, time that never changes.

My parents waited for me in the apartment of the retirement home where they live. They didn't really look much different than they had six months earlier when I had last seen them, although my father, who had chipped a bone in his foot just before my last visit, now used a walker. At 87, my father has black hair only slightly edged with grey. Seven years ago, at the dinner dance he gave for their sixtieth anniversary, he danced all night. He walked miles every day and then went out to play golf. Believing himself invincible, he imagined moving easily and forever that strong, healthy body. Old age was something that happened to other people until a bout with shingles, ill-managed by his physician, left him with severe nerve damage. In constant pain since then, he entered old age instantaneously, without warning. His own father died at sixty-three, so he had no model for old age. My mother, who is a year younger, is like a fragile, delicate flower, although her anger at finding herself insecure in her step, and tired, is anything but frail. "We should live and, when it's time to stop living, we should die," she says. She, too, never expected old age. "I don't know if I believe in God," my mother says, "but if she exists, she is not fair."

I didn't expect old age for them either. I have a sense of its possibility for me, but for them I accepted their myth. I am trying to understand the reasons for old age. There must be some. When life is not artificially prolonged, there has to be a use for those years. There was a time when old age was good for wisdom, when old people were sought for their wisdom. But my parents don't feel wise. They just feel angry at living too long. My father has an image of old age that revolves around generations of a family being together, the old folks sitting on the porch, secure in the knowledge that life is continuity, that the years are in order. I don't know where he got that image. I never asked him about his own grandparents. Did they sit on the porch of the farmhouse where he grew up? Who were they? How is it I have never asked?

My father wants to be honored as the patriarch. My mother wants to be left alone to read. People are never enough for my father. They are too much for my mother. Each is, separately, disappointed by life, dismayed to see what it finally becomes. Yet, sometimes I see them look at one another, their eyes so filled with the love and time and struggle, the wonder, the plans, the hope, and now the pain, the reality of sixty-seven years together, that I have to leave the room because I cannot explain to them why I am crying. Why, when they have each other in love, can they not embrace the end of life? Why is it so hard to embrace what is natural? Why are we so unwilling to take our place in nature, to enter, willingly, old age, death, the beginnings of life?

They thought it would be different. They thought they were magic, that life would deal differently with them, that they were not like other people.

In my father's pain, I see the physical manifestation

of all my own anguish. It is not unlike the process of healing I experienced at the hacksite. I guess I needed to be reminded again. It's as if my father had been chosen to make it clear for me, to teach me what happens when one abandons everything to one's pain. Pain is like some modern version of the devil, a version acceptable in an age when putting faith in a more literal devil is too big an anachronism for almost anybody. Like the devil, pain insists on your loyalty. It leaves no room in you for anything outside of you. You become servant to it. It becomes your god. You expect everyone to bow down before it and, in bowing, see how faithfully you serve. You pray to be released, yet cling to it at the same time. It has become all that you know. You have given your life over to it. If it released you, what would you have? You cannot live without it. Yet, you know that you cannot live with it. You are caught, trapped in your life, longing for a death that will not come. You must let go for death to come, but you cannot let go of the longing.

It strikes me as a great act of love for my father to teach me the necessity of letting go, even though I know he has not consciously chosen it.

Six months earlier my father was in a convalescent home waiting for his foot to heal so he could walk. His roommate was a one-hundred-year-old man who no longer had access to words. Trapped in a body that no longer belonged to him, he made sounds to express urgency—screaming and crying and moaning most of the night. In the morning the attendants dressed him and wheeled him into the hall for the day. The hall was lined with people without choices. They were all put there for the day, then wheeled back to their rooms at night. It was only in his twice daily physical therapy sessions that my father felt himself in a place he could comprehend. He spoke easily with the physical therapist who seemed a compassionate person. "I wish I had my old .45," he said to her at one session. A few hours later the floor nurse was on the phone to my brother telling him she was going to order a complete psychiatric evaluation to see why my father was so depressed.

"He's depressed because he's in pain and he's in that place and it's awful there," my brother said. "You'd be depressed if you were a patient there too."

"But he could be dangerous to himself."

"Did he say he would use anything but a gun?"

"No."

"And does he have one?"

"No."

"Then I suggest you forget about it."

The other day a friend told me about her aunt who, at eighty-two, felt tired one afternoon while ironing. She turned off the iron and lay down on the couch. She fell asleep. She died.

There are easy deaths. What dictates easy or hard? Why must some of us spend so much of the energy of our lives exploring the need to age and to die? The fight, the anger, the pain—they are all exploration—unwilling, perhaps, but exploration nonetheless. Those of us who do not yet understand enough to die are not ready to put the exploration aside. There is no easy route to understanding. I wish my parents the fullest possible understanding when it is finally time, yet I wish with all my heart they could be spared this hard route. While visiting my father in the convalescent home, and almost unable to bear his anguish—feeling able to bear anything but his anguish—I said to him that I would so gladly take his pain, if only I could. "I don't want anyone to bear my sorrow," he said.

Even his language is like mine, I thought as I drove home in the dark, warm night.

In spite of all this, our lives, on my visits, follow an easy routine. We go the places they need to go, do the errands they need to do. I work out in the building's gym and swim in its pool. The people who live there watch me swim and afterward they compliment me on it, and they tell my parents what a good swimmer I am, and we all feel good. We go down to the dining room every evening for an early dinner and the resentment I once felt at having to eat early—live on their schedule—has long vanished. What difference can it possibly make? I enjoy their company. We laugh. At night I sleep easily and long as if, even now, I am protected by the presence of my parents in the next room.

Yet, on this visit, I wanted to go home. I found myself impatient to leave, as if I were somehow impatient with their unhappiness. I could not understand my impatience. It seems to me that every minute with them is to be cherished. In one of those conversations we had while my father was in the convalescent home, I said to him that I wished I could stand the Florida climate so I could live nearer.

"No," he said. "We have had our lives. You have to have yours."

When, in my early twenties, I tried to come back home, he said to me, "Our house can only make you restless. You must find your own way now." They always knew it was essential to leave home. Only I was always reluctant to go. I was eighteen when I physically moved away, but perhaps the impatience I now felt was, at last, my soul's leavetaking. Perhaps after all this time on my own, I am finally ready to leave home.

Leaving home now meant going home. My home.

The north. I wanted badly to leave Florida and go north. It was instinctive, some act of self-preservation, an attempt to carry on although everything around me— my parents' anger at a hard old age; the loss to greed of open space; the denial of life both proferred; the endless hot, damp air—seemed to call a stop to life. When, on the flight home, I changed planes in Salt Lake City, I marveled at all the wonderful, dark, warm clothes people wore instead of the brightly colored, light materials of the clothes in the Palm Beach airport. I entered the corridor that serves as terminal for the Montana bound planes. It is downstairs and distant from the corridors where the planes to major places dock. The corridor seems small and dark and all the people waiting wore dark, practical clothes and waited in the dark, late night for their planes. It seemed the quintessential northern setting and I felt at home. When the plane landed in Bozeman, there was a light cover of snow on the ground. The air, smelling of winter, embraced me in its cold. An air easy to breathe, it does not press down against you. It does not enclose you. As we drove into town, I rejoiced in the small, dark town where winter filled the streets. A northern place, I thought, it is truly a northern place.

In the morning I took my dog for a walk up Bozeman Creek. It was snowing lightly, a soft, gentle snow. Not cold. Not bracing or windy or blasting challenges. There was much more snow on the trail and in the mountains than there was in town. It was pure and soft and silent. No one else walked there on that morning. I had come home.

Flowers

The Atlantic beats against the ancient granite cliffs rising straight and high and dark along the Maine coast. It is as if the continent itself was walled in, defended from the relentless force that would pull its land back into the sea. Exploding in roiling white spume against the rocks, the Atlantic pours over them to fall back in foam on the green edge of ocean. The spray shoots cliff-top high to lie in sea drops on our arms and lips and the black rock on which we stand. Lower down, the water glides over glossy, ocean-smoothed rock into dark and glistening pools. Where rock wall and ocean meet, rough waves surge into a narrow rock canyon. Trapped, they blast upward, spouting geyser-like into the sea air. Spouting Horn, this place is called. It is high tide. There is a wind, a rough sea; in the distance, a sailboat with lowered sails.

You believe you have some kind of power because you stand above the sea and observe. Then you taste the sea on your lips and you remember it and you know that, to the sea, you are nothing. The sea gives. The sea takes back. The land and all its life is temporary. On loan. Not to be taken for granted.

Spouting Horn is one of those places on earth where

it is perfectly clear there is no alternative to Nature; where its force, the force of oceans, of gathering storms, of tides and time offering neither succor nor consolation, presents us the fierce insistence of eternity. In the waxing and waning of tides is the whole story of life.

A twenty-minute walk from the ocean, on the inlet at Tenant's Harbor, Blueberry Cove Camp nestles in a gentle landscape, a place where meadow has been carved from the forest sloping down to the inlet. The inlet curves around Blueberry Cove. At low tide you can practically walk across it to the town of Tenant's Harbor without getting your feet wet. Tenant's Harbor is one of those old Maine towns with big 18th-century clapboard houses that look wonderful on picture postcards. Old Maine. Old New England. Quiet, serious, hard, strong, thrifty, steadfast, unwavering, quintessential America.

The camp, on the other hand, represents a kind of revolution. Not that revolution isn't as basically American as clapboard houses and parsimonious speech. It's just that, in this particular landscape, you don't see it a whole lot.

Founded in 1949 by Henry and Bess Haskell, Blueberry Cove Camp was the first for-profit interracial camp in the country. The Haskells believed so fully in the rightness of integration that they staked their livelihood on it. They also believed that if they could show integration as a money maker, others would follow their example. Although the camp caused a certain initial discomfort among the old guard Maine residents, in time they incorporated it into their lives. Still, revolution is not a one-shot deal. Either it begets revolution or it is nothing more than the status quo in the hands of somebody else. Change isn't revolution. Change is just change.

Partings

Painter Jon Moscartelo of the Blueberry Cove Foundation (and himself a former camper) approached Joe Mondello and Bruce Detrick of the Tamarand Foundation in New York City with the idea of offering a weeklong camp at Blueberry Cove for families with HIV positive children. For the Tamarand Foundation, whose mission is to bring nature and art to hospitals and to homes for children with AIDS, the camp offered the ideal, a chance to bring the children to nature instead of the other way around. The basic tenet of the Tamarand Foundation (named for Joe's six-month-old niece, Tamara, who died of AIDS, as did her mother, who was infected through a transfusion) is that life is nurtured by life. As Bruce says, "the spirit may be whole though the body is ill." For Henry Haskell, who is now in his 80s, and who lives down the road from the camp, the HIV camp—even though it was definitely not for profit—seemed a logical continuation of his work. In 1992, people's ignorance about those infected with HIV or AIDS is about on a par with their 1949 prejudices against blacks.

The timing of my first trip east in seven years coincided with the week of the camp. Bruce, who is my close, old friend, suggested that if I came up, I could help. Believing with all my heart in the work of the Tamarand Foundation, I had wanted to be of use for a long time, but there was little I could do from Montana. Blueberry Cove seemed an opportunity to help in the work, and do a favor for friends as well.

Bruce, Joe and I arrived at Blueberry Cove two nights before the beginning of camp. Parking the car in the fog that had been with us the whole trip up from New York, we entered the main lodge where Jon and the regular camp staff waited for us in front of a warm fire. Coming to a new place on a foggy night, when you cannot see where you are, is disorienting. You move through darkness to come to a place you have never been. In spite of the warm fire, it has no reference points. You know that everything will be different in the morning, but morning is too far away to be much use.

Yet, morning comes. In clear, bright day, without even the memory of fog, the camp director showed me the walk to the ocean. Following a dirt road lined with asters, blueberries and swamp maples, we passed a corner where a domestic garden marked the side road to someone's house. The garden was well tended, a mass of vibrant flowers, their colors doubly vivid in the midst of the dense and tangled greens backing away from the road, and the small, subtle flowers and berries that grow wild on this granite land. Coming upon the garden was like entering a sudden moment of light in a dark forest. The light is lovely, a gift, but it is temporary, the vision of a moment. When, one day, the garden is no longer tended, those flowers will be displaced by what is wild, what is natural to this particular piece of earth, what works here on its own. With the exception of the ocean, it takes a kind of subtlety to survive in this landscape. How different from the Rocky Mountains with their flamboyant wildflowers, although maybe in all that space, flamboyance is required to make a point. Here, on granite, closed in by greenery, it is enough just to grow.

About three-quarters of a mile up the road, we entered forest, its floor covered by dogwood and reindeer moss, a deep green and silent place. I forgot we were walking to the ocean until, suddenly, it was all there was ahead of us, steel-blue, white-capped, stretching from us to the sky. We stood on high rock headlands at the edge of America, the Atlantic crashing full force a hundred feet below.

Partings

By the time the campers and most of the staff arrived on buses that brought them up from Providence and Boston, New York and New Jersey, Blueberry Cove felt familiar to me. Most of the thirteen families were black; two were Hispanic; one was white. What all of them shared was the fact of a child, or children, with HIV. Some children arrived with HIV infected mothers; others with foster mothers or aunts because their mothers had died of AIDS, and with older siblings, children free of the infection. Besides cooks and a nurse with a direct line to AIDS pediatricians, the staff included musicians, naturalists, storytellers and, from Columbia Teachers' College, an artist and a dancer. The idea of the camp was to offer a little time out, a place to play, a safe haven where nature, art and music could provide a supportive and healing environment.

Healing. The dictionary says it means "to make sound; to cure of disease or affliction." Yet, even where curing of disease cannot happen, healing is possible. The aching heart can become whole. Any aching heart.

The campers, city people all, were led to primitive cabins, some without electricity, none with anything more than beds and perhaps a shelf or rough table. A few showers and bathrooms are scattered throughout the camp.

We had put a vase of wildflowers in each cabin, but nobody seemed to notice in the rush to change cabins because this one was too small or too dark or too lonely. The sorting, the unpacking, the moving in and out and in went on late into the night. When the campers interrupted their settling in to pour into the lodge for dinner, there seemed so many of them; tiny children and slightly older children, women carrying babies, a few teenage girls, some large boys. I sat at a table with Karen, her three-year old, Ty, her seventeen-year old foster daughter, Dee Dee, her friend Wanda, Wanda's five-year old nephew, Justin. Because I had already spent a little time with Karen and Wanda, I felt some familiarity. But I felt an intruder too, the white woman, the staff person, the outsider.

At the staff meeting called for 11:00 p.m., the first free moment, no one else seemed to share that feeling. At first I wondered if I had been in Montana for so long that the diversity of the east had become foreign to me. Yet, the staff was also a mixture of races and backgrounds and I was not an "outsider" with them. Was it simply guilt at being healthy in the face of so much illness? Guilt at being—so far—lucky? If that was so, why did the rest of the staff not feel it? How were they able just to launch into their plans for the week? Yet, what else could they do? Dwelling on the unfairness of life was hardly to the point. Even I know that. I tried to tell myself it was merely late. I was tired. I had had no experience with such a project.

It was a relief, after the meeting, to walk down through the woods to the tent where I was camped, a relief to be alone. Sleeping on the ground in the woods was familiar. I know where I am in the woods. The tent, out of sight of the camp buildings, provided me a privacy, a place that was my own. I treasured that place. Mornings, I woke to a view of forest ending at the inlet below; of tall, thin birches swaying in the wind, their shimmering leaves casting light that moved like water; of water in the inlet rippling against the shore, dappling the light that fell on it like quivering leaves. Now, at night, the tall shapes of trees reached into stars. I could hear the water swashing against the beach, and the ringing of the harbor buoys.

After breakfast the entire camp met to discuss the

day—according to Blueberry Cove custom—in a circle on the grass. On this first morning, as on my own first morning, the confusion of the previous night was gone. There was a sense everybody had moved in, the journey from fog unto morning repeated over and over. Small children and babies and the two Nubian goats that had the run of camp, walked around inside the circle.

Folksinger Nancy Mattila passed a smudgepot around the circle, offering its smoke to the Great Spirit as we all chanted, "the earth is our mother, we must take care of her. Hey yanna, ho yanna, hey yan-na...." Over and over we chanted as the smudge pot passed from hands to hands. A few of the children were self-conscious about lifting the pot and refused. Others did it shyly. The mothers and aunts lifted it for the littlest ones, their hands over the little hands so that even the babies could take part. Afterward, storyteller Christine Campbell, weaving a story out of all the threads that had come together in this place, presented us a common ground so that none of us were outsiders anymore. Nothing that happened in the circle, the interjection of a child, the sudden appearance overhead of an osprey, was left out of the story. In the soft Jamaican accent that filtered through all her plethora of voices, she incorporated the new into the familiar, offering us something magical, yet wholly believable. Magic. Truth. The right combination of outlooks to get through life, however long or short life turns out to be. It translates life to usable time, to the immediate moment. Allowing us to look at what is terrifying and come to resolution, it provides a context we can enter.

This is also what nature does, which is why using nature as a healer works. In nature, life goes from season to season, continuing forever. Even under the most adverse circumstances—a killer hurricane or unstop-

pable wildfire, earthquake, landslide, erupting volcano—
the earth picks up again and starts anew. The new life
forms may differ from the old, but the change they represent is the essence of life. I saw it happen in
Yellowstone Park after the fires of 1988 when the black
earth of burned forests suddenly exploded with color—
the gorgeous fuchsia flowers of fireweed and the brilliant
yellow of arnica. What joy the earth presented then!

Flowers. Wildflowers. Garden flowers. They form a
connection between one form of life and the next.
Intermediaries, go-betweens, they are like angels.
Children recognize angels. Some children probably are
angels. As we chanted in the circle, Jo-Jo, who is not yet
two, picked a yellow dandelion from the grass and
brought it to me. I put it in my hair. "Look, he's flirting
with her," his mother said to her friend. He took the
dandelion from my hair and walked away with it, his
baseball cap askew. Later, he came back and put his baseball cap on my head.

That evening Jo-Jo's mother had an asthma attack
and, in the morning, decided to return home. Dee Dee
brought Jo-Jo to breakfast while his mother packed. After
Dee Dee fed Jo-Jo, I took him so she could eat. He was
perfectly willing to be held by me. He had just come out
of the hospital. There must have been so many strangers
holding him in his life.

I showed him a bucket of cut flowers next to the
breakfast table; first a huge yellow, black-eyed susan at
which he simply looked, then an equally huge fuchsia
flower. He reached out to this one, touching it as if it
were his mother's face.

On a walk to Henry Haskell's house to pick blueberries, Ty, who had been sent along even though he wanted
to go with Dee Dee to a place at tide's edge too danger-

ous for the youngest children, sulked much of the way. The others, a dozen small black children running along the edges of perfect yards fronting large New England houses, were curious about everything. Only Ty, his arms just stretching around the huge berry bucket he insisted on carrying, seemed to look at nothing. He remained entirely inside himself until we came upon a pair of enormous wooden wheels in a yard—some gigantic old wagon hitch—eight feet high. He walked over to the wheels and rubbed his hands along the spokes he could reach. Soon after we turned off the main road onto the Haskell's road, Ty noticed a tall stem of white asters. He went to these and touched them. When I bent the stalk down so he could smell them, he leaned toward the flowers without a word. A few feet away were some purple asters. He saw these, touched them and smiled. Then he skipped down the lane, a child at last.

It is the healing force of nature with which Sarah Reynolds works through her organization, Animals as Intermediaries. She brings once-injured wild animals that cannot be restored to the wild to people institutionalized in hospitals and homes. On the floors of these places she builds environments of things she gathers in the meadows near her home in Concord, Massachusetts. And the people—imprisoned in illness, age and fear—find themselves freed to speak, to care, to enter in. Finding life, they live. What Sarah presents is the world before language, before misunderstanding. It is the world before loss.

Three boys and I followed her on a short walk through the woods as she showed us, by touch and smell, the differences in the barks of trees, the shapes of leaves and needles, the low plants, the high, the places a squirrel had been. The two boys who were older copied all that Sarah did, touching everything as she touched it. Three-year old Cory, meanwhile, wandered a little behind, engrossed in some adventure of his own until Sarah stopped at a patch of bright green moss and knelt to touch it. The two older boys touched it too, but quickly, perfunctorily. Cory sat down on the path next to the moss and ran his hand across it, pressed his hand down on it, into it, as if he would give himself entirely to this soft, yielding, gentle place in the forest. In the wonder on his face, I saw he had come to a magic place. Because I followed him, I had come there too.

A small girl, Shakia, brought me a story she had written on the bus from New York to Blueberry Cove. The story was printed in large letters on a single page. "It is fun to be on the bus," she wrote. "I am very happy." Giving her a notebook, I suggested she write a story every day so that, after a while, she would have a book. She beamed. I invited her for a walk to the high rock cliffs at the edge of the ocean. On top of the cliffs she sat bent over her notebook, so fully concentrated on her writing that I think she did not see the sea. Beyond her, the Atlantic rolled without stop into the cliffs, bright blue under a cloudless sky. High tide was past.

On the walk back, Shakia picked wildflowers along the road. As she picked them she showed me each new color and shape, then brought her bouquet to the lunch table.

After lunch, she gave me her story to read. "We went on a long walk," she wrote. "I am very happy."

I walked her back to her cabin for rest period. Two babies were already asleep in the double bed. Shakia carefully placed her notebook on the shelf next to the bed, quietly took off her shoes, climbed over the baby at the edge and slipped beneath the covers between the

Partings

two babies without waking either. I reached over to caress her face. Her dark skin was soft. It was like the softest silk. She smiled, then closed her eyes. I walked down to my tent and cried.

Meadow

The elk are bedded down. The meadow in which they lie is fresh with all the varieties of spring green. Bushes not yet in leaf make soft lines of mauve-grey. In the gentleness of evening, clouds in a white-grey sky press against the tops of mountains, wrap the mountains in their softness. In the cabins across Moraine Park there are no lights. I am alone here and night is coming. It comes slowly. It will be here suddenly.

A few miles away, in the town of Estes Park at the edge of Rocky Mountain National Park, people are taking evening strolls up and down the main street. They are looking into shop windows. They are buying ice-cream cones. I spent last night there and saw them doing it. Walking. Looking. In pairs, in families, in groups. They are not dancing. Only I am dancing. Here, in this cabin high up on the edge of Moraine Park where the elk are bedded down in the meadow, inside the sound of a dulcimer tape I bought in Estes Park, I am dancing out my sorrow.

The cabin once belonged to William Allen White, editor of the Emporia, Kansas Gazette, and confidant of Presidents. White fell in love with the area of the Park as a student, then built the house in those days when one could build a private house here. The houses across Moraine Park are also remnants of that era. The cabin was presented to Rocky Mountain National Park and now serves as residence for participants in the Park's Artist-in-Residence program. From the huge window that forms most of the west wall of the cabin, I look out at the Big Thompson River meandering down the meadow. Huge old ponderosa pines scent the air with vanilla, and make a park of the meadow. Scattered across it are boulders the glacier brought. Long's Peak is directly across from me and I can see the high peaks of Rocky—as people here call the national park—in the distance. I have been given time here to write. In return, I am to perform some service for the Park. (I will lead a nature writing hike for any Park visitors who care to come at the end of my stay.)

In the time I am here I will watch the light change in Moraine Park. Day and night I will watch it change, watch morning come and evening go, and record the light and wear it for my jewelry and not cry anymore for the beauty that is gone. I am at the beginning of twelve days in this cabin. Days come. Days fade away. The elk bed down in the meadow. Light slides along the side of the canyon. The pine tree outside the window does not move. Only the dulcimer makes a sound. And I dance. Remembering. In Montana, in February, I went to a ball wearing a dress of many colors and earrings that glittered like stars. Days after the ball, the man I danced with said, "You wore every color there is. And there was light at your ears." I remember how the dancing felt, awkward at first, and then floating, floating out into the night, the full skirt of the all-colored dress swirling out around me, me floating, he floating. There was a full moon and some soft warmth—almost tropical—that wrapped the night in ease. Clouds surged across the moon, then separated, leaving the moon near and huge and lighting up snow and heaven and the veranda where we danced, my skirt swirling about me, about the warm night, about the moon. I was beautiful that night, and I danced with a man who was beautiful, and I remember how the dancing felt. I will not wear the dress to dance again, or the earrings made of light, or be beautiful like that again, or dance again with that beautiful man.

Where does nature fit into heartache? Or is it the other way around? How can one feel so whole in nature and so ripped apart in the world of people? Why doesn't the wholeness last forever? How can you know a thing and then not know it? The wholeness is real. It's the other, the ripped-apart, that is to be questioned. Yet, one asks nothing of nature, so nature gives everything. One asks everything of a beautiful man, so one gets nothing. It's really quite simple.

Is that nature's pull? That it is the one place we can be where we ask nothing? Of course, there are people who ask of it—ask for its minerals, its trees, its rivers, ask to change it to something it wasn't meant to be, forests and swamps to farmland and shopping malls, deserts to suburbs, rivers to harnessed energy—and whatever other demands suit our insatiable need to use things. We who ask for everything will get nothing. One day. One day it will be used up. We will have used it up, poisoned it, torn it apart. And we will get nothing. Finally. It's only when we ask nothing that we are given everything. How foolish greed is. Greed is like the lover who cannot possess the beloved. "I possess you," a man I married when I was twenty said to me. Naturally, I left him. It is not enough to dance against the moon. We must possess the environment in which the moon hangs, possess the dancer with whom we dance, possess the earth, harness its light and, in doing so, destroy the freedom of our own movement across it.

What can I learn from twelve days and nights on the edge of Moraine Park?

Morning. It takes me so long to get started on a hike. Why am I so nervous about starting? I cannot figure out where to go because I cannot figure out where I am. Yet, I know I need to go in order to figure out where I am. It doesn't work the other way around for me. It never will. Guidebooks are no help. They only make me feel more stupid. How is it everyone else can figure out where they are going?

I should set out cross-country, leave the trails behind, wander without goals, without mileage counts, without maps. Yet I use trails, consult maps. I want to know the name of that canyon where the light hits, to know the names of the peaks that spread out behind the South Lateral Moraine. I want to know where I am in terms of names. I want to be able to say—oh, yes, over there, that's Long's Peak, that's Spruce Canyon. But if I never referred to maps, I could name them all myself and know them as well as I do by other people's names. The problem is, I think it's not appropriate to name a mountain without climbing it. It's no good just sitting around naming things. You have to be in intimate connection with them, feel, smell, experience them. You must taste a mountain as if you held its mud on your tongue or the cool, damp rock in your mouth. You must taste the bitter greens of wildflowers and the colors of blue and mauve and yellow in their petals; the sand grains and the roll of pebbles and the rough bark of dwarfed and wind-whipped trees; the clarity of sky and the heat of day that presses you tight against the mountain. Once you've climbed the mountain, you have some rights. Private rights. They have nothing to do with anyone else. Everyone else has private rights too. Everyone can call the mountain by his or her own name for it.

So I could only name these peaks if I climbed them. Maybe I will climb some of them sometime, but not now. Now I am supposed to be working. A short hike and time at the typewriter. Now I have to take the names already given to them, and I want to know where I am—on what trail, headed where, come from where, surrounded by what trees, what flowers and fields and rocks, what birds do I hear, over whose tracks do I walk?

It is the end of May and the high trails are still snow-covered. I make a short walk to Cub Lake in the clear morning and am home again as afternoon clouds over. The difference between today and yesterday is that now I begin to know where I am. It was an ordinary hike, easy, through some pretty country that smelled of pines and cold rock and, in one place, of summer meadow. Perhaps I expect too much of hikes. I expect them to be monumentally beautiful or to fill me with new insight—into wilderness, into myself, into the world. I expect connection with the earth or with myself or with some radiant moment. Yet, I am indeed different than I was before the hike, than I was yesterday. At Cub Lake, sitting against a rock, looking at the map with no anxiety whatsoever—because, now, at least, I was in the woods—I could see how the trails crossing the Park connect. I could identify the canyon I had watched last evening. Just an ordinary hike, but in making it, I have arrived in this place.

Rain falls in a fine mist, probably affecting nothing. I build a fire. The rain stops. The sun reemerges. Nine cow elk move out into the meadow to feed. Long's Peak

Partings

and Taylor Peak are covered by clouds, but between them the sky is blue. A cloud of white light descends into Spruce Canyon. An almost blinding light, it falls in bright rays—the rays of biblical illustrations—onto the meadow where the elk feed. Above the clouds the sky is blue. No one drives the road now. No one walks the meadow. It is a time for elk, for light, for silence. The light floods the room, falling through the big window, across the window seat and onto the wood floor. There is a wind that comes up strong at moments, as if to say whatever is now is only for the moment. Everything will change. Everything is as it always was. Nothing is permanent. Not rain, not sun, not light, not silence, not elk, not sky, not mountains, not the wind, not I. Perhaps people's urge to change things is the most natural of all. Perhaps we are all no different than all the other things of nature. We begin here. We end here. Neither beginning nor ending is permanent, yet both are eternal. This is not a new thought.

More rain and then a golden light, falling after the rain, falling onto the chair in front of the fire, glistening on the beads of rain in the pine tree, lighting this half of the meadow, falling gold out of an opening in the grey clouds, falling in a path across this table I use as desk and onto the tiger lilies in a vase on the coffee table, falling, fading, going, lying in a beam now straight from the hole in the grey-cloud sky to the fire in the fireplace.

Fourteen elk graze in the middle of the meadow. One runs back and forth, going from one elk to another, apparently trying to make one of the others run with her. First one, then another, then another. She runs back and forth along the herd. None of the other elk pay any attention to her. She stops, at last, and grazes. And now the golden light is gone.

Ms. Lillian's Bookstore

I had Thanksgiving dinner aboard the S.S. Taku somewhere on Alaska's Inside Passage. The dinner in the ferry cafeteria wasn't bad and everyone who bought turkey and trimmings got a free piece of pumpkin pie. By dinnertime, I had been on board the ferry twenty-four hours. Ketchikan, my destination, was still four hours away. Between Haines, where I had started, and Ketchikan, the ferry passed more miles of wild country than I had ever imagined. Deeply forested islands edged the steel grey water of the passage, their grey pebble beaches looking stark and northern and untouched by all but water and time. The solitary deer standing at the edge of one only made the land seem emptier. No, emptier is the wrong word. Wilder. What is wild is never empty. Sea birds skimmed low over the grey water. Sometimes the water's surface was broken by dolphins or a seal. We passed no other boats. No houses dotted the island shorelines. Except at the ports at which we called—Juneau, Petersburg, Wrangell—no roads split the forests that covered every inch of land I could see, or, at least, no roads that I could see. The land faded in and out of fog, rain, snow. Sometimes all sight of land disappeared in a broad stretch of water. I felt the immensity of wildness. It seemed primordial, a space beyond imagining, the geography of eternity. No wonder, then, that in its loss, we somehow lose our own salvation.

I was in the forward lounge reading John Muir's *Travels in Alaska* when we entered the Wrangell Narrows at Petersburg. I had just reached the part of the book in which Muir writes about the Wrangell Narrows, proving, of course, that nothing is by coincidence. I put the book down at once because I had been told by Ranger Zack in Haines not to miss the passage through the Narrows. Here, where the islands almost hug the ferry, a chain of buoys with red and green lights marks the only possible course for the boat. Many passengers stood at the windows. The Narrows, measure of the captain's skill, are a high-point on the trip. Most of the other passengers were Alaskans, bound for some part of the holiday with family to the south. Watching the ferry's passage through the narrow channel was a diversion on the long trip home.

Ranger Zack was the man in charge at the Chilkat Bald Eagle Preserve near Haines, where I had gone to do a story. During the time of the annual eagle gathering at the Preserve, from November through January, Zack tends to the visitors who descend on the Preserve in increasing numbers with extraordinarily expensive photography equipment. He takes care of any necessary law enforcement and observes what is happening among the eagles. Generally, the biggest job is getting photographers off the road—the only road connecting Southeast Alaska with the rest of North America—before they are run over by trucks. You can't really blame the photographers. It's not every day you see three thousand eagles at once. You want to get back far enough to get the big picture. Dressed in his park green uniform, his bearing reflecting the discipline of a military background, his body looking as if he does two hundred situps before breakfast, his face almost stern until someone asks him a question about eagles, or about the Preserve, when it lights up with eagerness to share what he has learned and what he loves, Zack is a handsome man.

Until recently, when he finally got an assistant, he had spent years as Chilkat State Park's sole employee, working summers as interpretive ranger, law enforcement officer and maintenance man. Probably more law enforcement officers and interpretive rangers should spend a little time on maintenance duty. Cleaning outhouses does keep one in touch with what is basic. Between seasons, Zack wanders around the world. The necessity to be alone wreathes him like a halo so that you find yourself wondering where his heart got hurt.

Zack was easy to interview for the story on which I was working. It was only when I was not interviewing him that he seemed shy, as shy, I suppose, as I am when not interviewing someone. When my hosts in Haines and he and I and a good many other people were invited to a party given by some filmmakers working on a video about the Preserve, Zack suggested having coffee after the party. But when he was ready to leave, I thought he had forgotten. "Am I still invited for coffee?" I asked.

"Of course."

We walked along the harbor from the party to the center of town where Zack lives in a small house overlooking the harbor and the British Columbia Coast Range. The high mountains, snow-covered, looked like huge blue cutouts against the clear black sky. The road along the harbor was icy, the snow framing it deep. Zack offered me his arm. Neither of us could think of anything to say. At his house we were greeted by a large blond dog. "This is Gus, the wonder dog," Zack said. The house was filled with souvenirs of Zack's travels—sculptures, baskets, art, implements, a smattering of the world's bazaars and marketplaces, an exquisite sensibility to what is integral to a people's life and vital to its art.

He made strong coffee and brought it to the sofa where we sat looking out at the harbor and the blue mountains beyond. The green curtain of light that had begun to dance across the sky as we had walked along the harbor now reached deeply down the sky. I thought that we could see it better if we turned off the lamps, but decided it might seem forward of me to sit in the house of a man I hardly knew and suggest he turn off lamps. Even at the time, I recognized this as an anachronism, but Zack seemed so proper. I didn't want him to think I wasn't.

"I don't mean to be improper," Zack said, "but we could see the lights better if we turned off the lamps."

The Northern Lights oscillated in full and marvelous drapery, filling the sky above the mountains, stretching down the vault of heaven, across the width of sky. We sat together on the couch and sipped our coffee and watched the play of shimmering green light. I marveled at the huge, cold beauty of the north. Zack seemed as engrossed as I. We did not talk. There was no need.

It seemed a long time before the lights began to pull back, fading, shrinking, receding into the sky that gave them birth. When they were almost gone, Zack turned the lamps on. Now we talked easily until there was a moment when there was nothing more to say. I left then and walked up the hill to the motel.

The next day I stopped at Zack's office with a few last questions for my article. That's when he told me to watch for the Wrangell Narrows. When I rose to leave he embraced me. I was surprised by his embrace, and even more so by its warmth.

Now, on the ferry, I thought about the way that embrace felt. Nice. Maybe I should consider the job I'd been offered at the Haines radio station. I actually liked Haines well enough to consider it apart from Zack. I liked the small, northern, winter feel of it; its place on the edge of the continent; a few extraordinary people I had met there; the fact of the Preserve and what its existence meant in terms of the environment. So it wasn't entirely a frivolous thought...not entirely....

The ferry docked in Ketchikan at 10:30 p.m. It was snowing. It had been snowing all day. The terminal was jammed with travelers waiting to board the ferry for the continuing route south and those who had just arrived from the north, rushing toward waiting relatives and friends, or joining long lines behind the couple of telephones on the wall to call taxis. If you could get through to the taxis at all, you were told they would send one in half an hour. Outside, in front of the terminal, groups of travelers argued with one another over whose taxi it was that had just arrived. Getting a taxi is a much politer event in New York City, I thought. It was over an hour by the time I arrived at my hotel atop a sheer cliff, no more than a few miles from the terminal. The hotel overlooks the town like a medieval castle.

The taxi made its way up empty streets to the steep, curving road to the hotel. The driver was nervous, unsure he could make it up the road in the new snow. "We're not used to snow," he said.

Morning dawned clear and crisply cold. From my window I could see the jumbled layers of streets descending the hillside of Ketchikan. At their end was the harbor, the Inside Passageway, the connection with the rest of Alaska. Outside, the air felt like a Montana winter day. "We're not used to the cold," people said to me often during the day.

A steep stairway leads from the hotel down to the topmost level of streets, which then wind into the main part of town. I followed it, beginning to get a sense of the town that had seemed so large to me on the taxi ride the night before. Night makes the unknown large. Or maybe night, presenting mystery, makes the unknown real, makes palpable the hidden spirit, the submerged history. These things are always large. Too large for the eye to encompass, they must be seen with the heart. The unknown frees the heart when what the mind cannot fathom is left to feeling, to the realm of heart. The unknown becomes, perhaps, the only essential knowing.

Superimposed on top of three native cultures—Tlingit, Haida and Tsimshian, as it is superimposed on the steep rock of the island where it sits, Ketchikan blends and separates the cultures of its land at once. What are the layers of time one crosses climbing from the harbor to the hotel? Whose are the layers of time?

The hotel, the Cape Fox, which belongs to the Cape Fox Corporation, the native organization responsible for a fair amount of tourist-related business in the area, amalgamates the layers. The Director of the Cape Fox corporation invited me to lunch. I thought it was to orient me to the area, but later I realized it was to screen me before an interview with Nathan Jackson, one of Southeast Alaska's most famous carvers, could be okayed. As a celebrity, he has, I was told, been made "use" of by journalists. He was no longer willing to give interviews without first screening the journalist.

I got the interview, but before talking to Mr. Jackson,

I visited Totem Bight, a park north of town where, among the mixture of Haida and Tlingit totem poles, is one of his. Although there are differences among tribes in the way the poles are carved, within those differences, native carvers follow prescribed forms. Totem poles are not a kind of individualistic art, yet the skill of the carver is very individual. Mr. Jackson told me that carvers exercise a certain amount of freedom. "You can tell by looking whose style it is," he said.

Mr. Jackson is a careful, gentle man. A dancer who once performed with the Chilkat Dancers from Haines, he is a Tlingit from the Chilkoot tribe, whose native country is the Haines area. His carving is also a kind of dance. The hand dances, the eye, the spirit. Wood is as alive as a dancer; carved, it receives new life, the mask, the costume, the ultimate revealing of its soul.

Is there then, some sacred duty in the carver's hands?

In Ketchikan's Heritage Center I felt so keenly the ancient soul of the massive totem poles rising in the enclosed center courtyard. Stripped now of color, softened, muted in form by time and weather, the poles are far taller and thicker than poles carved in recent years. They seem the ghosts of giant trees. Indeed, they are ghosts. Even in the Alaskan woods, for all the immensity of wildness I felt there—these huge, straight-sided red cedars have been largely lost to logging and development. The poles come from a number of villages and tribes within about a fifty mile radius of Ketchikan. In the silence of history, and some monumental ancient yearning of the wood, these poles rise now in the courtyard. They present a history of a place and its time, a history that weathers and rots and is replaced over and over by master carvers. Until now. Now, time is saved. Now there are museums for the salvation of time. Now, time is forever. In these totems there is mystery and knowledge, story and skill, the grandeur of the forest and the art of man. Outside, they would have weathered back into the earth, man's stories as much a part of the earth as man's bones. Here they are as much protected from reunion with the earth as man, dying, envaulted, is protected from the earth. We have found a way to study, to learn, to know. We have lost the way to the earth.

The Tlingit, Haida and Tsimshian elders of the region were asked "What is important?" before the mounting of the exhibit "This Is Our Life" at Ketchikan's Tongass Historical Museum. "Childhood, marriage, afterlife, trade, raven, the potlatch," they answered. "Life way back, going after food, carving, weaving, basketry, village, transportation, art today," they said. They did not have to say "It is the way to the earth that matters." The way to the earth is assumed. It is there in the objects displayed, there in the words of the elders presenting the meaning of the display to the public. In their words, I could hear their voices. I was in their presence, fully in their country.

How odd, then, to leave the little museum and find myself on streets that have nothing to do with Indian people; to find myself thrust into the white American frontier, into a history as insistent as it is recent. The shops I passed had windows full of Indian handicrafts and photographs of wild Alaska. If you don't let history get in the way, you can make it profitable.

Old wooden houses line Creek Street, the last of the wooden trestle streets that once comprised the town. The street backs up against the cold, wet rock of the mountain. Nestled against the rock near the steps leading up to one end of the street is Ms. Lillian's bookstore. Parnassus. "Bookstore, Café" the sign outside the small frame building announces. Inside, I climbed a stairway lined with books to enter, at the top, a small room also lined with books. In one corner there was a little cubicle with an espresso machine and a plastic case holding cookies and muffins. A couple of tables with chairs around them were placed in the center of the room. A grey-haired woman stood inside the cubicle talking to a man drinking coffee. I ordered a coffee and sat down. On the shelves around me the books were one of a kind, new books, used books, Alaskan books mixed in with books one might find in New York in some jumble of an old bookstore around Columbia or at the Strand.

    I had been in Montana for most of eight years. I had been looking for the café for the past twenty, a place to sit, surrounded by thought while drinking (good) coffee. The windows of Parnassus look out on the town below it and the bay. At 4:15 there was still a light glow in the sky, fading softly into a deep teal. Yesterday's snow lay on the streets. The lights of passing cars were reflected in the Ketchikan River as they crossed it on the bridge just past Creek Street. The sound of a classical guitar on tape wove in and out of the grey-haired woman's words and the fading light and the books that embraced the room. Her voice, with its slight sound of New York, was familiar. I felt at home.

    In my early years in New York, when there were still plenty of cafés, I spent my days at Figaro, sitting hours over an espresso and a notebook, documenting the life that passed through that door on MacDougal Street, the comings and goings of the regulars, the tourists, the artists, the hopeful, the fantastical, the lost, the crazies, the students, the trysters, tricksters, clowns, the bohemians, beatniks and assorted hangers-on in the days before fashion took over what had once been the province of art, the edges of art, the fringes of the world.

I filled up so many notebooks.

It was not until the afternoon that a friend sitting with me at Figaro said "you can no longer tell the artists from the bums," that I realized things were changing. I moved uptown. The artists went to Hoboken. I longed for the café, but could never again find it in America.

Until I came to Ketchikan.

Lillian Ference and her husband came to Ketchikan forty-four years ago. After her husband's death and her retirement, she opened the bookshop, the dream she had had for years. She filled the shop with books she liked. People coming to this place are served good coffee and good mind.

Ms. Lillian and I talked about books until closing time and then I walked out into the wintery night. It was dark. It had been dark for an hour. The air was like the air of Christmas, crisp and cold and pure. The streets wound and climbed and only I walked on them.

I went back to the café the next afternoon. Several people sat at one table, a man alone at the other. Ms. Lillian suggested I sit down at the man's table. The man told me he was working at a canning factory to earn some money, then return to his home on an isolated island on the Inside Passageway. He had lived on the island for several years, periodically coming into Ketchikan to earn money. When he had come out from California, there was a woman with him, but she had returned to California.

"Women who come here following a man don't stay in Alaska," he said. "Only women who come on their own stay."

By the time the phone rang, only Ms. Lillian, the man I was sitting with and I were in the bookstore. Ms.

Lillian answered it, then said, "Ruth, it's for you." This did not seem possible to me, but who am I to question what is possible? I took the phone from Ms. Lillian.

"Hello?"

"Brook?"

"This is Ruth."

"Is Brook there?"

"Just a minute. I'll see," I said, turning toward the man I was sitting with "Is your name Brook?"

"Peter."

"Brook isn't here," I said to the voice on the phone.

"Thank you, then. Goodbye."

I hung the phone up. "He wanted Brook," I said to Ms. Lillian.

"Oh, I'm so sorry," she said. "It was so nice to think you were getting calls here."

Peter and I spent a little more time talking about how to live in Alaska and then he left, and Ms. Lillian and I talked about books and life in Ketchikan. I left just before closing time, climbing the dark streets and the stairway back to the hotel. It felt so familiar to me now, as if I had been there for weeks. It felt the way it used to feel to walk along the winter night streets in New York on my way back to my apartment after a dance class, the streets swaddled in cold and me warm from class and full of movement; or the way it had felt to walk home in Paris after class at the Alliance Française. There was something about the streets, the winter air, the bookstore, perhaps, that made me a student, as if everything were yet ahead. It felt familiar enough that I wondered, for the second time in Alaska, what it would be to stay. Ms. Lillian had understood what it was to be at home here. She understood what it would mean to get a phone call at the café.

Esther

When the tall, slender woman with short grey hair entered the dining room, the room took on an aura of elegance; a radiance, as if a great ray of light had entered it. Dinner became an event possessed of the glitter dinner ought to have. The woman, Esther, always entered with George, the two looking as if they had spent a lifetime together. It seemed a lifetime of gentleness and of romance. On their way to the table behind my parents, they always stopped to talk a moment. If they were already seated when we came in, I stopped by their table after dinner. Esther always held her hand out to me, to take my hand, not in a handshake, but in a caress. Once she kissed my hand. It was a simple, loving act. This beautiful woman was filled with love.

She was perfect. Everything about her was perfect—her posture, her clothes, her jewelry, the radiance about her. Her radiance, allowing all things in, bestowed upon those things an elegance equal to her own. Her smile and warmth invited friendship with the world. There was about her an innocence, as if she could see only with joy, and the eagerness of a child. It was as if, in all her eighty-seven years, nothing bad had ever happened. Yet, at the same time, you knew this could not be true. No one could carry such enormous grace without understanding sorrow.

Esther's daughter and George's daughter, who are friends, had introduced the two of them when each had moved into the retirement home. They were a good match. At ninety-four, George is handsome, natty, possessed of a smile to equal Esther's. Esther was hard of hearing, but understood everything George said. When other people spoke to her, George repeated what they said, in a tone of voice no louder than that they had used, and Esther understood.

I looked forward to seeing the two of them on my visits to my parents. Then, an autumn ago, Esther did not always come to the dining room. "She's having problems with her back," George told me. On the nights she did come, she was as beautiful as ever, as loving, as radiant. Six months later, she did not come down at all. "She is very sick," George told me. "I don't think she can last much longer."

"May I visit her?" I asked.

"Oh, I know she would like that," he said.

She had been moved out of her apartment to lie in bed in one of the apartments the building holds for special care. A male nurse answered the door when I knocked. George came and brought me to her room. Esther's bed was in the middle of the room. She lay, slightly propped up, her eyes closed. She wore no make up and no jewelry. She was as pale as the white sheets and the white uniform of the nurse.

"I think she's sleeping," George said.

"Don't wake her," I said.

"But she would like to know that you're here," he said, then took her hand. "Esther, Ruth is here to see you."

She opened her eyes, although I felt that, open, they saw less than they had closed. "Ruth is here," George repeated.

"I just came to say hello," I said.

I could feel the force of energy she drew from some deep place inside to try to focus on me, to understand who I was and why I was there. Her eyes looked at me with every once of energy in her. I could see the question in them, the wonder.

"I don't think she knows you," George said.

"No," I said. "She doesn't. But there's no reason why she should. She never knew me well enough to know me now."

But George wanted her to know me. He wanted her to know I had come to see her. "Ruth. You know Ruth. She's come to see you."

Slowly, Esther lifted her right hand to me. I took her hand. "It was so nice of you to come," she said, the words drawn out, as if she spoke from some great distance. And then she smiled. Looking directly at me, she smiled with all the joy of all her smiles. Her radiance slipped over me, enveloped me. It was as if I were embraced by a kind of holy light. She did not know me as Ruth, but I knew she knew me as someone who cared about her.

"I just wanted to say hello," I said.

"I hope to see you again," she said.

"I hope so too," I said.

She held my hand a moment longer, her grip strong, and then she let it go and closed her eyes again.

"I'll go now," I said to George. He followed me out of the room. "I don't think she knew who you were," he said at the door.

"No," I said. "She didn't. But I'm glad to have seen her."

At midnight, lying in bed in my parent's guest room—which faces the front of the building—I woke to flashing red and white lights. I looked out the window to see an ambulance parked at the front door. For a long time nothing happened except that the lights revolved in circles over the drive and up to the fourth floor where my parents live. I watched for an hour until two attendants wheeled a stretcher out. Then it seemed to take a long time to prepare the ambulance to receive the stretcher. I could see Esther, her hand opening and closing on the cover over her. I thought she should not have to lie so long waiting, so exposed to the night or to the eyes of the windows. I watched until, at last, they lifted the stretcher into the ambulance. There was no one with her now but the attendants.

And me. I was with her.

The Big Drive

On a hot, dry September day, after a hundred years of Montana statehood, five thousand people gathered a short way from the town of Roundup for the start of the Great Centennial Cattle Drive. Horse trailers, trucks and covered wagons lined the staging ground parking area from one end to the other. Beyond the parking area, tents and tipis filled the hollows of a rolling landscape. Draft horses—huge, calm, magnificent—stood tethered to the wagons circling the tents. On the rolling hills behind the camp, riders exercised horses hauled long miles and hours in trailers. On a slight rise, the Montana Memorial Detachment, 7th Cavalry, Company K had pitched its tent. Company K was Major Reno's company, the one that got away from Custer's last stand. A 35-star flag flew over the cavalry tent. Cavalry officers paraded on their sorrel horses. In the dusty corral across the road, the lead herd of cattle, all of them longhorns, waited for morning, and the start of The Big Drive of '89.

For the six days of the Drive, this camp—the eighth largest town in Montana—would be packed up every morning, move on, settle in to the next site every afternoon. Each day's town evolved almost instantaneously, complete with a proper frontier bustle to its main street where horseback riders threaded their way among pedestrians—cowboys in long, sweeping dusters or leather vests, women in long, calico dresses, small children in sunbonnets, a nun, a mountain man or two. There were musicians, poets and storytellers who looked like all the other cowboys but held a different magic in their souls, or, perhaps, just a different—a more public—access to the same magic. The dusty street built in an hour held both a history and a present. At each camp a huge red and white striped tent erected by Budweiser functioned as saloon, dance hall, community center and opera house. The town had its own medical facilities and a daily newspaper printed on an 1840s press. Nighttime campfires in each wagon circle softened the hard, wide darkness of the prairie night, quieted down this monumental carnival bursting with its hundred years of energy and myth and eagerness for the West. No one is so eager for the West as the Westerner. He indulges in it as if it were some freeing masquerade, and yet, it is his own.

I was on the drive to write a story. I was really on the drive because I love cowboys. I have ever since childhood when my father, taking me to the western films he loved, thrust into my growing up a vision of that heroic, lonely landscape in which the cowboy rides forever into the sunset. Tall, lean, scarf knotted around his throat, big hat on his head, dusty boots, jeans worn from the saddle, mellow old leather chaps worn from the years, eyes mirroring a universal loneliness back there behind the permanent squint—he rides out on his good horse into eternal sunset.

I had always wanted to do it—to ride off into the sunset, tall and lean and weathered and tough and alone. I wanted to be that cowboy I loved. I wanted to understand aloneness to the depths of my being. I wanted to feel loneliness so hard that it would be like lying on the baked summer Montana earth or leaning against the rock of mountains. I wanted the solitude of hermits and of saints...but according to my own myths, the myths my father gave me. I could see myself riding into the sunset. I could feel it.

There was only one problem. I didn't know how to ride a horse. Actually, the problem was deeper. I was terrified of horses. When my father tried to teach me to ride at the age of two, the horse seemed so large; I so small; the distance to the ground so far. My father didn't press it. I grew up afraid of horses, and longing for them. When I moved to Montana forty years later, it was clear that learning to ride was now or never. After that horse packing trip in the Bob Marshall, I registered for Beginning Equitation at Montana State University.

The horses ran kicking and bucking into the school arena. My stomach did the same thing, but it was too late to turn back. If I left the class now, I would never ride a horse. I told the instructor about my fear and he assigned me Babs Barmaid, a wonderful mare who is sort of a special for cowards. Babs did all she could to help me. While the rest of the class chased their horses across the arena to catch them, Babs walked up to me. She practically put the bit in her mouth herself. Anything she could do to help, she did. Allowing me to believe I was in control, she taught me control was possible.

Before the Great Montana Centennial Cattle Drive, I had had time to take the beginning class a second time, the intermediate class once, and go on a couple of pack trips through Yellowstone. I had been on a few horses besides Babs and I believed absolutely that anything you wanted to do as much as I wanted to go on the cattle drive had to be possible. I forgot I was scared of horses.

I borrowed a horse named Tess from some people in Kalispell and drove up there a couple of times before the Drive to ride her, then arranged to meet her—and her owners, Jan and Jim, at the staging ground.

The first evening in camp I saddled Tess, Jan saddled her horse and we rode out beyond camp. All around us men and women loped their horses across the hills so that riders and horses and hills all seemed part of the same thing, some absolute moment of life and movement and endless time. Here, in a great group fantasy, was the white history of the West; the present reestablished in a past that belonged to us all.

Suddenly I realized where I was and what I was doing and I got scared. Here were five thousand people obviously born in the saddle. Four thousand nine hundred and ninety-nine. How could I have imagined I could do this? What if I did some stupid thing and fell off my horse in front of them all, got trampled out of stupidity. I do not want to die out of stupidity I wasn't really worried (for the first time) about getting injured or killed. I just didn't want to be embarrassed. But there was nothing I could do about it now. Except ride.

The first dawn was clear, and already hot. My fear hadn't lessened, but now there was an excitement curling around it, holding it the way a mother holds a baby, or a lover the beloved. If the fear was me, I felt protected by the excitement. And, for the moment, distracted by the movement of the camp. Jan and I sat on our horses at the fence, near the gate through which the train would roll. Across the road, a few of the 105 cowboys there to drive the cattle herd waited with the lead herd. When the corral gate was opened, the cattle surged

Partings

through onto the narrow road, cowboys flanking them and behind them. The cavalry, its 35-star flag hoisted at the front, followed—off to a far surer victory than it had probably ever known out here. The wagon master shouted—"Wagons...Ho!!" and they began pouring out of the gate—covered wagons, buckboards, surreys, one after another after another, their proud, beautiful teams swirling up the soft Montana dust in this immense moment of absolute belief in the hope and possibility of the American West. Three thousand three hundred and thirty seven riders followed the wagons. The rest of the 105 cowboys drove the main herd over a different route than we would travel, but would end up near the wagon train camp. Twenty million people could be fed by the trail herd if it was converted to hamburger, I was told.

We entered Roundup. Thousands of spectators lined the street, shouting out their excitement, their pride and support. I felt them riding with us, but I also felt immense to be riding, as if I, myself, had suddenly become bigger than life. I hadn't thought about that, about being a part of the parade, about what it would feel like to ride a horse down a corridor lined with thousands of cheering people.

Out of Roundup the wagons settled in to some rhythm of the road, riders to the heat and the crowds, horses into the hot ride surrounded by thousands of strange horses, shying from time to time when they got too near a wagon. Odd, these horses would all have been comfortable around a motorized vehicle, but most of them had never seen a wagon before.

At the first camp I met The Cowboy. He was holding a press conference to answer questions the accompanying reporters had after the first day's ride. I stood at the back of the group of journalists circled around him. He was tall and easy and used to being handsome. Engaging with each person who asked a question—about the logistics of setting up camp, securing the horses, providing water enough for so many people and animals, maintaining medical facilities, law and order, entertainment—he really looked at them. He listened. He didn't rush. He had a kind of time about him. None of the questions the journalists asked had occurred to me. I just wanted to ride my horse and smell the dust. On the other hand, I looked at that man's eyes, and knew I had to ask a question. Any question. The conference seemed to be over. The journalists began to drift off.

"What do you think of the drive so far," I asked.

"It's a miracle that a place like Montana exists where something like this can happen," he said, looking fully at me now. Dark brown hair curled out from under a tall, brown hat. He smiled. His blue eyes laughed. The creases in his face emphasized his ruggedness.

"Tell me about Montana," I said.

"This drive will let the world know Montana exists," he said, "and let Montanans know they matter," he added, referring, I supposed, to the fact that somewhere along the way the drive organizers had decided this was too big for Montanans to handle and brought in an out-of-stater to run the organization. It was an act not uncommon in Montana where people think that if a Montanan does it, it won't be as good as if someone from somewhere else does it. The result of bringing in the outsider was that the Cattle Drive almost didn't happen. The man probably knew about organizing political campaigns—that was his background—but he knew a good deal less about horses than I did, had probably never seen a long-horn cow, a covered wagon, a cowboy who wasn't in a movie. He had never ridden or walked across this land of sagebrush and cactus, of rolling, dry earth. He could have been anywhere, for all he knew. You can't come to Montana like that. In Montana, you have to know where you are. You have to know you are in Montana.

At the last moment the man was dumped and the floundering drive was taken over by Montanans who pulled it together with the sheer force of their immense energy and will. The Cowboy, one of the original organizers of the drive, had opted out when the outsider was brought in. With the outsider out, he came back. He was, in fact, not a cowboy, but a cartoonist, one of two cartoonists who had put the whole thing together. That seemed right to me. There was a way in which this whole thing was one huge comic strip where whatever role any of us assumed had its place—humor, adventure, romance, pathos—something clearly drawn that could be played out across the course of years, something one could depend on, something that, one way or another, was part of all our lives.

There was nothing more to say. I introduced myself and held out my hand to him. He held it a long time.

One day and night on the trail was all it took to make us feel the drive as a way of life. By the following morning it seemed as if we had been traveling like this forever. How quickly one gets into routine, providing it is the right routine, the routine natural to one's temperament and one's soul. It suited me—walking across camp in the early mornings, watching the camp wake, a few horses being exercised in the soft mist, dry dust rising up to mingle with mist. A cowboy walking down the camp road, his long duster sweeping back behind him, appears like a vision out of the mist. The sounds from the chuckwagon tent lure him in. The earliest risers sit on bales of hay outside the tent, mugs of steaming coffee in their hands against the early morning cold. Sun filters through mist, through dust. The quick heat of day spreads over the camp, moving now, with tents being razed, wagons loaded, corrals broken down to be piled on the flatbed truck that will take them to the next camp. Horses whinny to one another. A man, seated on the edge of time, plays a harmonica. It is full day and the train is on the trail. Thousands of horses are on the trail. The rolling sagebrush country is alive with riders and horses and cattle and wagons and a hundred years of dreams. This dream we are having is no different from the early dreams. We are no different from the early dreamers. No matter who tells us otherwise.

When, at the very end, the routine changed, all of life changed. On the last night, at camp not far from Billings—Montana's largest city—the camp was opened to people not on the Drive. They came by the thousands to have a piece of it, and to watch the big country/western show planned as a finale. The headlights of cars from Billings and probably half the other towns in Montana formed a chain that ran for miles, as far out along the road as you could see. These crowds would not see the real life of the Drive. Their appearance cancelled it. The line of headlights cancelled it. The rows of parked vehicles, the big stage with its spotlights and loudspeakers, the aura of fairgrounds cancelled it. You couldn't blame the visitors for wanting in. And you couldn't blame the drive organizers for having planned the event. After all, the drive was for Montana, not just for the few thousand people who had participated the whole way. The few thousand people were for Montana too. It was just that we were somehow surprised by being thrust so adamantly into the present. It was as if we were

Partings

blinded by the lights so that all that had been our lives for the days of the Drive faded into some darkness where we could not see. We knew the Drive would end. Yet its ending caught us off guard. Many of us stayed to ourselves, back, away from the lights, clinging to the last, to the time that was ours. But you cannot keep endings from happening. They happen. If you cling, you cling to what is already gone.

In the early morning, horses, riders and wagons lined up for the parade into Billings, the grand finale. In a sense though, we had already had our ending, already left the days of the Drive, the intensity of history. The Cowboy stood near the gate to the road, holding out his hand to those who passed. "Thanks for coming," he said and smiled, the warmth of his smile making each person feel as if they, personally, had been of utmost importance to the Drive, to The Cowboy, to the history of Montana. "Thanks for coming," he said to me, as he held my hand, again, a little too long. Not long enough. I rode on through the gate next to Jan.

It was a short ride to town where spectators, standing on curbs, on vehicles, on top of trailers, on top of roofs, lined the route. They shouted their greetings, their triumph. Signs in shop windows, hoisted onto roofs, draped across vehicles welcomed us, and we rode in as if it were a triumph; as if we had been coming a long time, across a great distance.

For me, it was a great distance. I had ridden fear two thousand miles across America in order to come to this place where I could ride Tess into Billings. It had taken me more than forty years to do it. It was worth every mile, every minute of the time. After all, I was heading into the sunset all the way.

Stopping near the stockyards, we sat on our horses

and watched the cowboys bring the herd in, keeping them within the confines of the roadway. They came like a river, a river of longhorns, relentless and without end. They, too, had come a long way, ushered into the end of the 20th century after a hundred years coming across the plains. The cowboys had not changed in all that time. The cattle had not changed. We had not changed. Billings had changed. The road was paved and people who lived there had cars and trucks and television sets and special arrangements had to be made to close the streets so the cattle and wagons and riders could come through. We stood and watched, our watching our goodbye to the huge beautiful fantasy the Drive had been. The wagons, the camps, the horses, the cowboys, The Cowboy, the poets, the dust—all a dream, all gone now, all eternally present. In ending, the dream became fuller than ever. What endings do is let you know the thing itself was possible.

With the last of the cattle past, traffic resumed on the street. We turned and rode back out to camp where the horse trailer would pick up the horses. We rode with the traffic, to the side of the road. The road was no longer ours. We had become peripheral. We stopped for red lights. We crossed the parade route and rode up the country road back to camp. There were other riders along with us and some going the opposite direction. An occasional vehicle passed on the country road. The Drive was over. I had done it. I had not fallen off my horse. I had forgotten I was afraid. I had entered that childhood my father gave me.

Cedar Key

The grey water of the gulf laps against the pilings of the pier opposite where we sit. Pelicans roost on the pilings that extend up from the pier. Waiting for a fish to fight for, they gather on the pier in small flocks between the fishermen lining both sides. A cormorant floats by on the water below us. Several gulls fly over, their cries piercing the grey air and the gentle lapping of the water. A day of rain; the sky lies on the horizon as grey as the water.

There was a double rainbow at dawn. Daniel called me out to see it. I imagined it boding well, although I should know by now you can't make assumptions about rainbows.

We sit on the railing of the long, narrow balcony edging a funky old bar built on a pier. The pier extends out from a curve of the island so that you feel you are at the edge of things; the land at the edge of the earth; land's end; the beginning of the oceans that circle the earth. Out there, ahead of you, is one very large baptism. The rain lets up, although the sky remains grey. Low golden rays of sun slide through a parting in the clouds, shimmering like sheets of gold against the grey. The gold pours out of grey sky onto the sea, the fishermen, the pelicans. It washes over the rusty old fishing boat moored at the end of the pier. It spills onto the balcony where we sit so that we, too, are bathed in gold. Perhaps it is the gold the rainbow promised. There should be a double amount of it, although I suppose one could hardly ask for more than this gleaming sky now offered. Yet it seems almost a mockery, a sort of consolation prize, as if the universe would say to me—"You cannot have your foolish fantasy, so take my gold instead. Grab this gold before it fades, or you will lose it too. Rejoice in the moment of beauty, the instant of light. Do not ask for more because there is no more."

The barman brings us our drinks.

"I need to be by the sea," Daniel says. "I've always had this longing. I'm at home when I come to the coast. I need to stay here for a while. I know when a place feels right."

"It's how I feel about Montana."

"For me, it's the sea."

"What are you telling me?"

The water laps without change. The fishermen on the pier barely move. The pelicans roost, huge beaks pressed against their chests, shoulders hunched against the sky. Rooted to their posts, they seem ancient birds. Primeval. Suddenly, wings flapping with the immensity of effort required to leave the earth, a pelican heaves heavily into sky, then dives like a bomb into the water and comes up without a fish. He floats, as if his only intention had been to reach the water. The sea suits him. It supports him. He does not look ungainly floating on it, as he did lifting into sky. The sea supports so many oddly designed creatures. It makes way for them. It surrounds them. Holds them. And moves as if they did not exist.

Partings

Nothing stops the sea. It is always moving, lapping at shores, caressing shores, battering them, building them, tearing them apart, carrying them off, delivering them elsewhere, devouring them, restoring them. Rising, falling, the sea alters the beaches from day to day, inexorably changing the land. The land is no match for it. The sea gives birth to the land and its creatures. It reclaims them. All powerful, all consuming, it draws them to itself. Daniel is no different than all the creatures of the sea. He follows its lead while I cling to earth far enough inland that I think I am safe. We connect in passing, tossed together like fish rolled shoreward with the tide. Wrapped in shimmering gold light, we have a drink on this pier and watch the grey water.

The North American Open

On the flight from Anchorage to Fairbanks, the plane passed by Denali. The afternoon sky was clear, the mountain dazzling, heaving hugely into heaven, its corniced arêtes and massive faces blinding white, the snow wind carved and pure. I know people who have waited weeks at Denali's base for the clouds to lift, waited so long for even a glimpse of what I saw so fully on my first trip into Denali's country. Maybe the pilot was actually making a slight turn as we passed, but I thought he dipped his wings. I wondered if he was a climber.

Hannes met me at the Fairbanks airport. We have been friends for more than twenty years, but had not seen one another for the past nine. Nine years earlier, ready to make a permanent move from New York, and needing to decide whether it would be to Innsbruck, Paris or Montana, I visited Innsbruck. I had once lived there, which is where I met Hannes, a mountain guide who now runs the largest mountaineering school in Europe. On that last trip, I understood that, for all that I loved the Alps, I could not do without the wildness of Montana. I need to live where there are grizzly bears.

On that trip, Hannes had looked as he had always

looked, a bear of a man, barrel chested and robust, his black hair and beard full, his body ready to leap into whatever physical challenge offered itself, his whole persona commanding, fully aware that no one could help but do his bidding. It was not a vanity, this awareness. It was simply a fact.

Although I knew I had changed in nine years, I expected that he, like any major monument, would look the same. I thought of him as a landmark, something one could count on. When I did not see him at the gate, I wondered if neither of us recognized the other, but all the people meeting people seemed accounted for. Walking down the hall to the stairway to the entry floor, I wondered if, in German, I had misstated the day or the time. At the bottom of the stairs, I noticed a slight, older man sitting by himself. Tanned, weathered, bearded. But too old. Too thin. As I stared at him, he rose and came toward me, his smile as open and perfect as it had ever been, his eyes filled with their tremendous warmth. In his embrace was all the power I remembered, but I felt how thin he had become. Lean. There was nothing there but muscle. Nothing extra. This was Hannes stripped away to the bone. The essence of the man, as if he pushed luxury away from himself, as if he no longer had time for excess.

Hannes had been in Fairbanks for a month. He and his son had arrived via Lufthansa Cargo from Frankfurt with about thirty sled dogs and all their paraphernalia. The dogs were in wooden box kennels that could be transferred to the back of rented trucks. This was their second season in North America, the first in Alaska. They had been in British Columbia the previous year. As we drove from the airport to the apartment Hannes had rented, we were both awed by the fact of seeing one another in Alaska. For each of us, just to be in Alaska is immense, a dream as big as the country. To be there together constituted an act of magic. That we had worked out the timing in letters and phone calls was irrelevant. Like all true meetings, it had nothing to do with plans.

Hannes and his son had both raced in the weeks before I arrived. His son, who was nine when I last saw him, had flown back to Europe a few days earlier to return to school, taking his own dogs with him. Both men race sprint dogs, dogs bred for speed over relatively short distances, a very different kind of racing from long distance events like the Iditarod or Yukon Quest. His son races in the unlimited class, which means any number of dogs above ten. Hannes races in the eight-dog class, mainly so that he will not compete with his son. He was now left with eleven dogs, three of them eight-month-old puppies he had bought in Alaska.

At the apartment, Hannes served coffee and muffins. *Pause,* it's called in Austria—the hour one sits down to coffee and pastry, maybe at home, more likely in some lovely café with marble tables and racks of newspapers against a wall. In Fairbanks, he had bought a big box of mixed muffins in the supermarket. The muffins were actually not bad. We sat together on the sofa with coffee and muffins and had a chance to see who we were. We had had the drive to get used to one another; to remember. Now we could look. Neither of us was young anymore. This is something you do not notice by yourself. You cannot notice it with people you see daily. You require someone who represents time to understand it. Even then, its not yourself you notice, but seeing the other, you understand that you, too, have come through time. When you see it, what you discover is that you have known this person a long time. Your lives are separate, but your histories entwine. They hold together like the hands of lovers, letting go and picking up again. You see how much the other has changed, and know you have changed as much. You know he sees it too. You cannot hide. Here is someone who has known you and who knows you still. What he sees at first is the difference, and then what he sees is the love he feels, and the same thing happens for you, and you know, then, you are with a friend.

You do not want to hide. You want to be who you are, but you want it known that once you were beautiful. No one I meet now will ever know how I looked when I was twenty-six. But Hannes will always know that. In those years, Hannes photographed me on the tops of many mountains. I still have the photo he took of my first rappel. I am wearing his hat. I see the fear on my face, and yet, I am calm with an absolute knowing that Hannes will not let me fall. Hannes taught me trust.

He taught me to climb. On my first climb I had a hard time with the second move, but when too much time had passed, and I knew I had to either move or quit, I moved. After that, that particular climb was easy. Hannes was on top, belaying me. I was safe in his hands. There was no way I could fall. Knowing I was safe kept me from falling. I loved the rock. I loved the feel of it under my fingertips and my boots, the feeling of solidity offered by the most delicate holds. I loved the closeness of the rock to me, feeling so personally the difference between shadow and sun. I moved as quickly as possible through the cold places of shadow; lingered, if the holds were big enough, in places of sun-warmed rock. I loved the form of rock. It seemed, on one hand, so unyielding, on the other, always ready for my body, if only I would take the time to see where it would hold me. Sometimes I mixed up which was rock and which was Hannes.

Hannes had been climbing since he was a child. From our first meeting, I wanted to be Hannes. I wanted to climb as he did. I wanted to understand mountains as he did. I wanted to run up them with his joy and his knowledge. I would watch him climb ahead of me, then copy his moves. After that first climb, I was never afraid, so long as I was with Hannes.

I had not experienced that before—to be never afraid. It was what allowed me to trust him so completely. There was nothing I could not do with him. He took care of me on mountains and he took care of me off mountains. He took me home to his family and made me part of it. I never knew whether he was my father, my teacher, my lover, my friend, my mentor. There was no way to define what he was for me. I guess there was no reason for it either. There still isn't.

In a restaurant in Fairbanks, we sat in big armchairs at a table opposite the fireplace. The waitress knew him. He and his son had come here a few times. "Order for me," he said. "Anything. Just don't tell me."

At first, knowing how particular he is about what he eats, I felt it was too much responsibility although, almost at once, I was pleased he felt I could take care of him. I remembered how hard it always is for me to order from an Austrian menu, and my German is not bad, while his English is rudimentary at best.

It was interesting, having the language tables turned. In Austria, although he always tried to include me in conversations, he would inevitably get caught up in them with whoever else was there and leave me behind. Unless people were speaking specifically to me, it was often hard, in a group, for me to keep up. Somewhere along

Partings

the way, the language got too fast, too foreign and I would opt out. Sometimes, seeing what had happened, he would bring me back in. Sometimes he would just let me be until we were either alone again, or with his family. Now, although he had picked up a bit of English, he could in no way enter into a conversation between two English speaking people. I translated for him until the point where I got caught up in what was being said and forgot to translate. I had never before seen him out of the center of things. For me, Hannes had always been the center of the world.

Although he was not racing in it (the event was for the unlimited class), we planned to be present at the North American Open, one of the major races for sprint dog racers. It is a three-day event, with mushers running over a 20-mile course each of the first two days, 30 miles on the third day. The race begins and ends in downtown Fairbanks. The racers need assistants to bring the dogs to the waiting sled, clip them in, see that lines are not tangled, hold the dogs back until the start whistle. Eager for the race, the dogs can barely keep their feet on the ground as they wait. Hannes was helping one of the racers with whom he had become friendly. I felt how hard it is to be competitive, and not to be competing. You *know* what it feels like to take off in a race, but you are one of the ones not doing it. Still, to assist, at least, gives you a reason to be there, keeps you from being part of the crowd, a spectator. Being a spectator feels so helpless, as if life were a vicarious event, one you cannot enter. Although I like watching races—horse races, human track events, ski races, dog sled races—I am always resentful that I am not among the running. I don't think it would make much difference to me which role I played—human, horse or dog—I just want to be running. So, the feelings I lay here on Hannes are suspect. I felt bad for him because I hate being out of the running.

"Is it hard not to be racing?" I asked him.

"Yes."

He wanted to do some business, to buy some more dogs. I went with him to the house of George Attla, an Athabascan dog sled racer who, at 59, is a year younger than Hannes. Attla has won the North American Open eight times. As he left this year's start, one leg furiously pushing against the ground to gain speed, a man behind me shouted, "Watch him, he's gonna haul ass!" He was probably talking to a companion, but I felt he was shouting to the world. "Watch him!" When Attla took off and when he came into the finish, enormous cheers went up from the crowd—much of which was Indian—on both sides of the street. Competing against the best racers in the North American, most of whom were young enough to be his children, Attla came in ninth, but nobody looked like him at the start or finish. Nobody stood so tall, so proud as this lean and weathered man.

Attla's cabin sits at the edge of a clearing in the forest. In the clearing, about 60 dogs were tied in front of their kennels. Another 20 were tethered to a large dog truck parked between the kennels and the cabin. Lingo, the lead dog who had won so much with Attla, lay listlessly inside his kennel. Old, sick, in pain, Lingo cannot live much longer, but Attla was having a hard time with the idea of putting him down. They have been through too much together. A huge portrait of Attla and Lingo hangs in the living room of the cabin. In the portrait, both of them are young.

Hannes is curious about the Indian. Although they are radically different men, there are similarities in their age, in the wiry leanness of their bodies, in the immensity of their pride and their huge ability to focus. Both of them like winning. Hannes would have liked to talk more intimately to the man, to know him better. But when language is limited, you use it for the necessities. It was enough for Hannes to conduct business. To do even that, he was dependent on me—with Attla; with another racer from whom he hoped to buy dogs; with the shop where he wanted to buy a large supply of a nutritional supplement for the dogs that is outrageously expensive in Europe; with the vet to whom he took one of his dogs when the dog developed an abcess.

It was odd—to find him dependent on me; to find him smaller than he had been; to see his face, in spite of his amazing eyes and that brilliant smile, so much older. I was pleased that I could, at last, pay back a little of his caretaking of me over so many years, but it was hard, too, to find him not entirely in charge, to find him in need of help, to find him somehow physically diminished, even though I knew his slimness was deliberate, born of the need to keep in top form as an athlete and of his distaste for self-indulgence. I felt a sadness about him. To some extent he voiced it. If he were younger, he said, he would live in Alaska, but it seemed to him out of the question now. I guess it was that that saddened me; that he had come to a place in his life where there were limits. I am younger enough to still insist there are none, but have to wonder if that is, finally, what aging means. Will I come to the place where Hannes is? Must I learn there are, indeed, limits?

We drove out to the dog sled trails just outside of town. From the parking area on the flat valley floor, you can see the Alaska Range and Denali standing like some blue dream miles and miles away; out there, at the edge of the earth. So the earth, too, has its limits. Yet, here,

Hannes was as he had always been. With the sleds and the dogs, he was at home.

He pulled his sled into position, attached a second one behind it for me, laid out the gangline to which the lines that clip onto the dogs' harnesses are attached. It was like watching him uncoil a climbing rope. He dropped the sled's anchors, then pulled each dog to its place in the line. It was like watching him fix a belay. Once the dogs—Magic, Curry, Bazil, Dog, Vinnie, Conn and Lace—were clipped in, he brought Preis, his lead dog out and clipped him in, told me to jump onto the runners of my sled, stepped onto his own, lifted the anchors and we were off. The sun-dappled trail wound through birch woods and conifers, across open meadows, through all that was glorious and right. Hannes, me, eight dogs, running through the middle of Alaska, the dogs, tongues hanging out, smiles on their faces; me, hanging on to the sled for dear life; Hannes, skimming along with his hands behind his back. When I saw him with his hands behind his back, I decided this was easier than I thought it was, and relaxed my grip. Now, I moved more easily with the sled. Hannes turned every few minutes to make sure I was all right, turning so quickly back that I was unsure he had really checked. But I knew he had, as he always had on a mountain. He moved with me through Alaska the way he moved with me up a mountain, unobtrusively making sure I was all right, yet expecting that I would be; then pressing forward with his great eagerness, his enormous appetite, his magnificent confidence, the comfort of knowing he was in his rightful place.

Here, I thought, is Hannes. He is who he has always been. Only we are both older, and everything has not been easy.

Partings

We left Alaska on the same day. Me first. At the airport he said, "I'll be home about eleven. Will you wait for dinner?"

"Yes, Hannes, of course. I'll have dinner ready."

We had no language in which to say goodbye.

The Christmas Bird

There was a hard wind blowing on the morning of Christmas Eve; a big, melancholy wind that bowed the bushes and bent the tree limbs against the grey light of morning. I was trying to pretend it was all right to be spending Christmas Eve alone—I had never done it before—but it wasn't all right. This, the part of Christmas I most loved, I had always shared—with family, friends, husband, lover. I was angry at finding myself alone. And frightened. How had this happened? Is this what my life would be now? I was resentful at being left out of the joy of Christmas.

I watched the wind much of the morning. While I watched the wind, a small bird fell down the stove pipe and into the wood-burning stove. The bird must have taken shelter on the edge of the stove pipe under the little metal roof fitted above it, then been blown off balance by the wind. There was no fire going in the stove at the time. If there had been, the bird would never have perched on the edge of the pipe. I discovered what had happened when I found my dog sitting in front of the stove, staring at the glass doors as if he was watching television. Not that he watches television. I don't have a set. But if he did, that's what it would look like. When I noticed him sitting like that I stopped to see what he was seeing and heard the bird inside the stove. The doors were too smoked over to see much, although I heard a tremendous amount of movement and then, as the bird hit up against a door, I saw its dark shape and flapping wings.

If I open the door, I thought, the bird will fly out. My dog will chase it. If the bird is injured, he will probably catch it. If the bird is all right, it will begin flying around my house. My ceilings are high. There is no way to catch a bird up there.

I hate birds inside houses. Everything about them changes when they are inside. Symbols of freedom outside, *inside*, they become both prisoners and jailers. Incarcerated, they wield power. As a child, I knew some people who had a canary that flew freely around their house. Visiting them meant putting yourself at the disposal of that small, yellow darting thing that could do anything it liked. You were completely at its mercy. It had a control I could not counter. We were not evenly matched, that canary and I. It's no wonder I love raptors—birds that soar and dive and do not waste motion flitting from place to place. An eagle or a falcon would be all right, but I did not want the bird in my woodstove in my house and I did not want to deal with it by myself. Not wanting to deal with it alone was not good for my self-image, but it was a fact. It was enough to deal with Christmas Eve by myself. I was not interested in final straws. Sullenly, I dialed Animal Control.

Connie, Bozeman's animal control officer, had come to my house several times to pick up stray dogs that had followed me home from the park and to deal with the skunks living under the garage. She had once asked if the dog she was picking up could keep the rawhide bone

I'd given him. She really cares about the dog, I had thought, liking her enormously. But she's probably not there on Christmas Eve, I thought now, listening to the phone ring. "I'll let her know," the officer who answered said.

It was not long before she arrived. Listening to the now silent stove, she gloved up, opened the door, fished around in the ashes and pulled out a small bird, all grey and limp. Had it died in its thrashing, or had it mortally injured itself in its fall? I had no idea what kind of bird it was. It was so little and so grey, so softly dead. Connie took it away with her. And I mourned it, poor little bird, blown by the morning's fierce wind into the stove chimney, falling in terror all those dark feet of the chimney, struggling in the ashes, dying when there was no reason for this day to be any different for it than any other day.

Years ago, in New York, I saw a man hit by a car on Fifth Avenue, in front of Lord & Taylor. The man flew through the air, arcing upward before landing some feet ahead of the car. His glasses, jolted from his face, flew ahead of him. They landed a few feet ahead of him on the ground. I have been haunted ever since by the idea that the man had not expected, when he got dressed in the morning, that he would die that day.

I left the house for a few hours, thinking about the little bird all the while. I returned to find my dog sitting in front of the woodstove. I heard thrashing inside. I called Animal Control. When Connie arrived, there was no sound from the woodstove. Nor was the bird to be found inside, either alive or dead. A wild goose chase, was all I could think of, feeling foolish. A wild little grey bird chase. As soon as Connie left, I heard the bird in the stove. I called Animal Control at once, hoping they could reach her on the radio before she got very far. She returned shortly, although this time with an assistant. It occurred to me that she didn't bring the assistant to deal with the bird. The bird was not in the stove when they arrived. Speaking slowly, with great patience, as if English was not my native language, the assistant suggested placing a large garbage bag over the stove entrance so the bird would fly into it and I could—she said—then easily catch it. The assistant inserted a board vertically to hold open the mouth of the bag. The two of them helped me tape the bag over the entrance and left. As soon as they were out of the driveway, the bird entered the bag.

The end of the bag bounced around as the bird fluttered and jumped inside. I started to remove the tape on one side when I realized that I needed both hands to remove the tape and close the bag at the same time, which meant I had no way to keep the board from falling. It seemed to me that when it fell, it could easily hit the bird. After the bird and I had been through so much, I did not want to hit it on the head with a board. But if I pulled the board out first, there was no way to avoid providing a moment of opening through which the bird could fly. I need help, I thought, knowing that even I could not call Animal Control again.

My next door neighbors, Bruce and Frankee Muller, proprietors of the Voss Inn—a very beautiful Victorian bed and breakfast—used to run a photo safari lodge in Botswana. Before he got involved with tourism, Bruce was a game warden in Botswana. They are the best of neighbors. Surely I could ask for help. Leaving my dog closed up in the bedroom, I went next door. Bruce came over a short time later. The bird, of course, was no longer in the bag, or, for that matter, in the stove.

"Call me when it comes back," he said.

As soon as he left the bird returned. I called him at once.

"I'll be right there," he said. I went back to the room with the stove to find the bird, a little brown wren, sitting on the pot of water I keep on top of the stove to keep the air from drying out. It just sat there, calmly, looking at the room. I decided to close the few doors in my house so that if it flew it would, at least, be confined to the main part of the house. While I was doing that, the bird flew to the top of the wood pile where it stood until Bruce arrived, at which point it dived behind the wood pile. Quietly, gently, log by log, Bruce moved the wood.

"It's easier dealing with elephants," he said. "You can't lose them in a wood pile."

When there were only a couple of logs left, Bruce reached down behind them. The bird screamed. Bruce got both hands around it and gently lifted it from its hiding place. In his hands, it was quiet. I held the door open and he carried it outside. He opened his hands and the little bird flew into the huge, old blue spruce in my neighbor's yard. It flew, without wavering, into its life.

Later, I made a fire in the stove and my dog and I ate dinner in front of it. The room, my house, were bathed in a radiance I had no need to question. Alone on Christmas Eve? Hardly.

Takashi

In a few days Takashi will leave the farm in Kumamoto for a couple of weeks in India. He will return at the beginning of spring. "I am eager to work in the fields after doing no physical work all winter," he wrote me. "Spring will come with cherry blossoms," he continued, "just after the equinox here, the time of green fire."

Green fire. The blooming of the earth. The beginning. The new year, new growth, new hope, the renewing of life. Takashi sees the spread of green across the earth like the spread of wildfire, relentless, inevitable. He also sees the revolution necessary at this point in history if that green fire is to spread anew each spring forever. I don't think he sees himself as a revolutionary, but I do; one of those quiet ones who can wait centuries if they must; one of those who people follow so that, ultimately, their work is done. I know he sees a time frame shorter than centuries. He thinks more in terms of ten years, or, if not quite so soon, then, at least, in the lifetime of his nineteen-year-old daughter.

The revolutionary act required is that of embracing the earth, honoring it enough to leave off poisoning it, finding a way to make its life healthy and sustainable.

Not a big deal really, when you think about it. Most people would probably prefer not to poison themselves and their homes. On the other hand, a great number of people don't seem to have a problem with poisoning their children and grandchildren if they can make money at it. It's probably not really deliberate. They just can't imagine an earth unable to do their bidding, or a priority ahead of material success. Takashi, an organic farmer, a writer and a holy man, believes the days of those people are numbered. Once they are gone, once their children take over the care of the earth, we will enter a time when green fire will truly spread across the earth. In Takashi's presence it is possible to believe in that time.

I listened to Takashi speak at a church in Bozeman. "This is the earth," he said, drawing a circle on a blackboard. In the center of the circle he drew the figure of a man. "And here is man at the center. Many people believe they are at the center of the world." Then he drew another circle, and put man along the line of the circle, a part of the circle, a part of the earth, a part of nature.

And the whole view of the earth changed.

He held up a large Japanese advertisement in which the earth is shown receiving an injection from a hypodermic needle. "Some people think the earth can be saved by an injection from outside, but this will not work. It can only be saved from inside. The change must be from inside the earth. It must start from inside each person. It does not come from society. There is no society. There are only people."

On his farm, Takashi produces what he needs to eat and what is necessary for the restaurant his wife runs. As all farmers do, he watches the seasons, understanding the earth must die, must go through the darkness of winter in order to come to spring. There is no escape from the darkness if the earth is to be reborn.

"Spring comes slowly," he said, "one little piece of green at a time, but, in the end, everything is green."

A week before I heard Takashi speak at the church, his close friends Cliff and Joan brought him to my house for dinner. They had become friends when Cliff and Joan spent a year in Kumamoto. Afterward Takashi had come to Montana to teach a course at Montana State with Cliff, a soil scientist. The course focused on the sustainability of the earth. When I heard about the course, I wanted to take part. There was something in it I needed to learn. I was welcome to sit in, Cliff told me, but by then the class would meet only twice more. I decided too little was more difficult than nothing and let it go.

Now, a year later, when I called Cliff and Joan to invite them to dinner, I had no idea Takashi was visiting. After he came to my house I thought how it is that the guest is invited, even when we do not imagine his presence. Nobody comes into your life by chance.

After years in India, in monasteries, begging on the street as a holy man must, trying to understand his own connection to the earth and, through himself, man's connection, Takashi's eyes laugh and dance. At dinner he drank wine and ate meat and entered into the conversation. His voice was quiet. Sometimes it was hard for me to understand his words, but I was at home with him. He could have spoken any language.

In the days that followed I went to listen to him speak several times. His English became familiar to me. At a meeting at Cliff's house of the class he and Takashi had taught, I watched a young woman listen to him. Although she sat quietly, I could see her whole being reach out toward Takashi, as if she leaned forward and stretched her arms toward him. "I listen, I read, I think I understand," she said when Takashi had finished talking. "But I never become wise. How do you become wise?"

How beautiful she was with her black hair and white skin and her yearning for wisdom. But what if there is no wisdom? What if there is only life, and the intensity of one's connection to it? Will life disappoint her if that is all there is? Is she me? Do I watch my own yearning? Is the longing for wisdom an abstraction that offers safety? Perhaps the person who is most wise is that person who enters most fully into life. All life. There is no difference between the life of the earth and the life of each individual. The difference is in how we respond to the connection.

Takashi and I spent hours talking in my house. He brought green tea grown on his farm. We drank green tea and talked about green fire—the earth and the book he is writing, the result of the course he and Cliff taught. Takashi's book, a philosophy, a plan, a hope, a vision, is meant for students, young people who still have time to see themselves as part of the earth rather than apart from the earth. In the book Takashi talks, among so much else, of his six years in India. He had gone to India in the 60s as everyone had gone then, hot on the tail of some drugged out Nirvana. But he had remained, searching, although he did not fully understand his search until its answer appeared. "It was Mother," he said. "When I saw her, I knew what I had been looking for. I asked her what it was I was to do. 'You must have compassion for others,' she said."

Is this universal spirit Takashi found—the nurturing spirit he names Mother—the source of wisdom or the call to life? Mother. A friend of mine who moved to Oregon from Montana wrote me that "Montana feels so like my mother." A psychic I once visited out of curiosity told me I had had to come to Montana to be born. My own mother, angry at God, had referred to God as "she." Mother is a complicated word. It is what sets you out there in the world, expels you out of darkness into light. No one will ever demand so much of you again.

One evening Takashi and Cliff and I went to a zen meditation. Afterward Takashi said to me, "Do not focus on your breathing. Meditate with your heart." When he said that, I felt the immensity of my heart, as if it filled my entire body. I could feel it grow in me and push everything else aside. It seemed a heart that I could use.

The day before he left for a week in California en route to Japan, Takashi brought me flowers—iris of the deepest purple I have ever seen, and lilies of a soft, vibrant yellow; the colors of holiness and of sun, of midnight and a summer afternoon.

Flowers must be so beautiful because their lives are so brief. If something is only going to be around a short time, it better have the means to get its message across fast. The message of Takashi's flowers seemed clear—the message of beauty is beauty, of life is life. The chain of iris, of lilies, the renewing, sustaining chain goes on forever. Death is a sidetrip. Life is eternal.

We sat with the flowers and drank green tea. When it was time to go, Takashi embraced me, his kiss ardent, warm, a goodbye, yet not a kiss of parting. It seemed a seal on work we would do together. There was love in it, a love whose source is the spirit he calls Mother. "When you need me," he said, "think of Mother. We will meet in Mother."

In this parting, there is no distance. The miles between us are no more than a detail. Japan. India. Montana. All details. Only the earth is not a detail. When he left, I continued sitting with the flowers. The iris lasted a few days. Some of the lilies wilted a couple of days after the iris. Two lilies, each on a separate stem, stayed fresh until he reached Japan. When they died, I took them outside and laid them in the garden.

Afterword

In April, my dear, old friend Marty Luray was diagnosed with cancer. By early June he was dead. Marty, who gave me my first writing job, had read *Partings* in its early stages, becoming most involved with "The Poet." Do we somehow know the stories of our own lives before the stories are ever written?

He wrote to me in May. I could not answer him at once. One evening, after listening to a tape of songs about love and friendship, I was able to cry. I wrote to him the next morning. He never got my answer.

5/12/93

Dearest Ruth,
I have wanted to write to you for many days and evenings, but I seem to get more tired as the shadows progress although on the glorious evenings we had last week it was just to sit down without staring for minutes into empty space. I seem to do a lot of staring into space. I am not sure what I am staring at.

We are at a juncture now where I have requested my oncologist to find out if there are any programs I can fit into at the National Cancer Institute. It is a last ploy in which I have little faith and when I look into the eyes of this nice man, I know he has little faith in it either. But he is willing to try. The oncologist at Mass General, an avowed aggressive chemotherapist, advises me to get my affairs in order. I do that. I get my affairs in order. That little part of me that is not in denial, arranges for a cemetery plot by the sea, makes certain bequeathals, certain music for the funeral and then, having done its job, dives back into the black depth that keeps me from thinking clearly about this.

We have talked about it, you and I. You asked me about the state of my soul. My soul is mostly intact. It is like a gopher; appears and perches on the side of its hole on those golden days when the water is close to my ankles as I sit on the steps of the seawall and I close my eyes and hear the eternal waves form their hollow cylinders and crash and the stones move as they have forever.

I wonder what happened to me. I wonder what happened to me in such an extreme way that it is almost like an execution. I find that very difficult to understand, which may be the source of my denial. The person who goes before a firing squad doesn't realize what is happening until they put on the blindfold.

I am still trying to puzzle all of this out, but I know that talking with you (as always) has helped me see things more clearly. We have had this relationship that never really needed a lot of words in order to communicate. My greatest regret is that we were unable to see each other over the past nine years.

I started this letter on Wednesday. On Thursday the latest door was shut; there are no experimental programs at NIH that would accept me.

Nicholas Monsarrat's wife found these words among

his notes after he died. They seem fitting, somehow.

"Let me end my days somewhere where the tide comes in and out: leaving its tribute, its riches, taking nothing. Giving all the time, pieces of wood, pieces of eight: seaweed for the land, logs for the fire, seashells for pleasure, skeletons for sadness."

My love to my oldest true friend.

Marty

6/4/93

Dear Marty,

How hard it must be to write the letter you wrote to me; to tell a friend the doctors say there is nothing to be done; how hard to write something that there is no way to comprehend. How could there be anything on earth harder than to be given the information you have been given. Out of the blue. For no reason. Except it is....

How do I respond? Disbelief? Anger? Refusal to accept what is unacceptable? How is it even possible to talk about what is happening? It seems so preposterous...I am so angry....

Last night, listening to a woman named Kate Wolf sing a song about friendship, I was finally able to cry. I think I was crying for all that love can never do. My love for you as my friend cannot make you well. It cannot change the course of life. It can't do anything at all but be. It seems so futile, yet I think that "being" is probably the one thing that survives our passages between lives. None of us know how long we are given. Most of us don't get the opportunity, while we are still of strong mind, to put our affairs in order, which is probably easier than facing what seems so arbitrary a death sentence. Yet, to have the time to take stock, to see where we are and to make the plans we want to make, seems a kind of gift, albeit a difficult and terrifying gift.

What can I do to help you? You help me so much by writing the letter you wrote; by calling me your true friend. You are my true friend too. There is so much I could never have managed without you. I would not have been a writer without you. What would my life have been without you...?

I think of you, dear friend, and I love you.

Ruth